Aileen Osborn.

40 E. 36 St.

N.Y.

OPEN SESAME!

POETRY AND PROSE FOR SCHOOL-DAYS.

EDITED BY

BLANCHE WILDER BELLAMY

AND

MAUD WILDER GOODWIN.

Volume I.

ARRANGED FOR CHILDREN FROM FOUR TO TWELVE YEARS OLD.

————o•o§•o•oo————

BOSTON, U.S.A.:
PUBLISHED BY GINN & COMPANY.
1898.

TYPOGRAPHY BY J. S. CUSHING & CO., BOSTON, U.S.A.

PRESSWORK BY GINN & CO., BOSTON, U.S.A.

PREFACE.

"OPEN SESAME!" a collection of poetry and prose for school-days, has been prepared with the hope that it will encourage children, first, to learn by heart; secondly, to learn things worth learning; and thirdly, to learn these things because they like them.

In this volume will be found some of those simple words by which little people may come to know great authors, — Shakespeare, Ben Jonson, Dryden, Addison, Swift, Gay, and Cowper; Byron, Scott, and Burns; Wordsworth, Coleridge, Keats, Southey, Campbell, and Lamb; the Brownings, Thackeray, Dickens, Ruskin, and Charlotte Brontë; Tennyson and Swinburne; Bryant, Longfellow, Emerson, and Lowell; Schiller, Victor Hugo, and many others. Here, too, are favorites, new and old, which, while of less famous authorship, have been stamped "classic" by the verdict of childhood. Some selections which appeal to children on the emotional rather than on the intellectual side have been admitted upon the theory that children may thus be led on from things valuable in sentiment, and pleasing in expression, to those of the highest literary quality.

Certain poems, both fine and familiar, which would have a natural place in this volume, will be missed from it. The editors regret that, in spite of diligent effort, it has not been possible to secure their use.

The book is illustrated wholly by engravings from the old masters, in the belief that children will enjoy and profit by the best art as well as the best literature.

The hero of the "Arabian Nights'" tale found the words, "Open Sesame!" a charm which revealed a rich treasure, and his talisman has been borrowed as the title of these volumes, with the wish that they may prove an "Open Sesame!" to the treasure-house of literature.

The editors extend their cordial thanks to the following publishers and authors, whose generous co-operation has made the collection possible, and whose contributions appear in this volume: —

To Messrs. Fords, Howard & Hurlbert, for selections from the writings of Henry Ward Beecher; to Messrs. Roberts Brothers, for poems by H. H.; and to Oliver Ditson & Co., for Christmas Carols from Rhymes and Tunes.

To Mr. Richard Watson Gilder, Mrs. Margaret E. Sangster, Mrs. Annie Douglass Robinson, Mr. Richard H. Stoddard, Mr. Charles Henry Webb, Mr. James Whitcomb Riley, Mr. Thomas Wentworth Higginson, Mrs. Emily Huntington Miller; to Right Reverend Bishop Doane; and to the literary executors of Gen. J. W. Phelps, Mrs. Ethel Lynn Beers, Mrs. Elizabeth L. Prentiss, and Mr. William Cullen Bryant.

Selections from the writings of Longfellow, Whittier, Emerson, Lowell, Celia Thaxter, T. B. Aldrich, and Margaret Deland are published by business arrangement with Messrs. Houghton, Mifflin & Co.

TABLE OF CONTENTS.

TABLE OF CONTENTS.

xi

SENTIMENT AND STORY.

FROM A PAINTING BY ANDREA DEL SARTO.

SENTIMENT AND STORY.

GOOD–MORNING.

ROBERT BROWNING.   SONG FROM " PIPPA PASSES."

THE year's at the Spring,
And day's at the morn;
Morning's at seven;
The hill-side's dew-pearled;
The lark's on the wing;
The snail's on the thorn;
God's in his heaven —
All's right with the world.

A LEGEND.

R. H. STODDARD.

THE young child Jesus had a garden,
    Full of roses rare and red :
And thrice a day he watered them
    To make a garland for his head.

When they were full-blown in the garden,
    He called the Jewish children there;
And each did pluck himself a rose,
    Until they stripped the garden bare.

"And, now, how will you make your garland,
   For not a rose your path adorns?"
"But you forget," he answered them,
   "That you have left me still the thorns."

They took the thorns and made a garland
   And placed it on his shining head,
And where the roses should have shown,
   Were little drops of blood instead.

POOR LITTLE CHILDREN.

Victor Hugo.

MOTHER birdie stiff and cold,
   Puss has hushed the other's singing;
Winds go whistling o'er the wold, —
   Empty nest in sport a-flinging:
     Poor little birdies!

Faithless shepherd strayed afar,
   Playful dog the gadflies catching,
Wolves bound boldly o'er the bar,
   Not a friend the fold is watching:
     Poor little lambkins!

Father into prison fell,
   Mother begging through the parish;
Baby's cot they too will sell, —
   Who will now feed, clothe, and cherish?
     Poor little children!

HOW THE GATES CAME AJAR.

FROM THE ITALIAN.

IT was whispered one morning in heaven
    How the little child-angel, May,
In the shade of the great, white portal,
    Sat sorrowing night and day.
How she said to the stately warden —
    Him of the key and bar —
"O angel, sweet angel! I pray you,
    Set the beautiful gates ajar —
Only a little, I pray you,
    Set the beautiful gates ajar!

"I can hear my mother weeping;
    She is lonely; she cannot see
A glimmer of light in the darkness,
    Where the gates shut after me.
Oh! turn me the key, sweet angel,
    The splendor will shine so far!"
But the warden answered: "I dare not
    Set the beautiful gates ajar," —
Spoke low and answered: "I dare not
    Set the beautiful gates ajar!"

Then rose up Mary the Blessed,
    Sweet Mary, Mother of Christ:
Her hand on the hand of the angel
    She laid, and her touch sufficed;
Turned was the key in the portal,
    Fell ringing the golden bar;

And lo! in the little child's fingers
  Stood the beautiful gates ajar!
In the little child-angel's fingers
  Stood the beautiful gates ajar!

"And this key, for further using,
  To my blessed Son shall be given;"
Said Mary, Mother of Jesus —
  Tenderest heart in heaven.
Now, never a sad-eyed mother
  But may catch the glory afar;
Since safe in the Lord Christ's bosom,
  Are the keys of the gates ajar;
Close hid in the dear Christ's bosom,
  And the gates forever ajar!

GOOD CHEER.

CHARLOTTE BRONTÉ.

LIFE, believe, is not a dream,
  So dark as sages say;
Oft a little morning rain
  Foretells a pleasant day.
Sometimes there are clouds of gloom,
  But these are transient all:
If the shower will make the roses bloom,
  Oh, why lament its fall?
Rapidly, merrily,
  Life's sunny hours flit by;
Gratefully, cheerily,
  Enjoy them as they fly.

THE ROSE UPON MY BALCONY.

W. M. THACKERAY.

THE rose upon my balcony, the morning air perfuming,
  Was leafless all the winter time and pining for the
    Spring.
You ask me why her breath is sweet and why her cheek
    is blooming,
  It is because the sun is out, and birds begin to sing.

The nightingale, whose melody is through the green-
    wood ringing,
  Was silent when the boughs were bare and winds
    were blowing keen.
And if, Mamma, you ask of me the reason of his singing,
  It is because the sun is out and all the leaves are green.

Thus each performs his part, Mamma, the birds have
    found their voices,
  The blowing rose a flush, Mamma, her bonny cheek
    to dye;
And there's sunshine in my heart, Mamma, which wak-
    ens and rejoices,
  And so I sing and blush, Mamma, and that's the
    reason why.

NESTS.

JOHN RUSKIN.

MAKE yourselves nests of pleasant thoughts! None
of us yet know, for none of us have been taught in

early youth, what fairy palaces we may build of beautiful thoughts, proof against all adversity; bright
fancies, satisfied memories, noble histories, faithful say-
ings, treasure-houses of precious and restful thoughts,
which care cannot disturb, nor pain make gloomy, nor
poverty take away from us; houses built without
hands, for our souls to live in.

"ELIZABETH, AGED NINE."

MAGARET E. SANGSTER.

OUT of the way in a corner
    Of our dear old attic room,
Where bunches of herbs from the hillside
    Shake ever a faint perfume,
An oaken chest is standing —
    With hasp and padlock and key —
Strong as the hands that made it
    On the other side of the sea.

When the winter days are dreary,
    And we're out of heart with life,
Of its crowding cares are weary,
    And sick of its restless strife,
We take a lesson in patience
    From the attic corner dim,
Where the chest holds fast its treasure,
    A warder dark and grim:

Robes of an antique fashion —
   Linen and lace and silk —
That time has tinted with saffron,
   Though once they were white as milk;
Wonderful baby garments,
   Broidered, with loving care,
By fingers that felt the pleasure
   As they wrought the ruffles rare.

A sword, with the red rust on it,
   That flashed in the battle-tide,
When, from Lexington to Concord,
   Sorely men's hearts were tried;
A plumed chapeau and a buckle,
   And many a relic fine;
And all by itself the sampler,
   Framed in by berry and vine.

Faded the square of canvas,
   Dim is the silken thread —
But I think of white hands dimpled,
   And a childish sunny head;
For here in cross and tent stitch,
   In a wreath of berry and vine,
She worked it a hundred years ago,
   " Elizabeth, aged nine."

In and out in the sunshine
   The little needle flashed,
And out and in on the rainy day
   When the sullen drops down plashed,

As close she sat by her mother —
The little Puritan maid —
And did her piece on the sampler
Each morn before she played.

You are safe in the crystal heavens,
" Elizabeth, aged nine,"
But before you went you had troubles
Sharper than any of mine.
The gold-brown hair with sorrow
Grew white as drifted snow,
And your tears fell here, slow-staining
This very plumed chapeau.

When you put it away, its wearer
Would need it never more, —
By a sword-thrust learning the secrets
God keeps on yonder shore.
But you wore your grief like a glory;
Not yours to yield supine,
Who wrought in your patient childhood,
" Elizabeth, aged nine."

Out of the way in a corner,
With hasp and padlock and key,
Stands the oaken chest of my fathers,
That came from over the sea.
The hillside herbs above it
Shake odors faint and fine,
And here on its lid is a garland
To " Elizabeth, aged nine."

For love is of the immortal,
    And patience is sublime,
And trouble's a thing of every day,
    That toucheth every time;
And childhood sweet and sunny,
    Or womanly truth and grace,
In the dusk of the way light torches,
    And cheer earth's lowliest place.

A BALLAD OF ST. SWITHUN'S DAY.

E. H. HICKEY.

THREE little noses are flattened against the pane;
Three little rosy mouths are bemoaning the rain;
Saint Swithun is christening the apples with might and
        with main.
"O Saint Swithun, Saint Swithun," the children say,
"Surely you've christened the apples enough to-day."

"Rain, rain," say the children, "be off to Spain!
Never, never, we charge you, come back again!
We want to run in the garden, and down comes the
        rain!
O Saint Swithun, Saint Swithun," the children plead,
"We want our run in the garden, we do indeed.

"Dear Saint Swithun, our lessons have been so long;
Dreadful sums, Saint Swithun, that would come wrong!
We wanted to dance a little or sing a song,

And now we are free, Saint Swithun, we're kept in-
    doors,
For, because you are christening the apples, it pours
    and pours.

" Good Saint Swithun, our lessons are over and done ;
Kind Saint Swithun, we're longing to take a run ;
When you were young, Saint Swithun, you liked some
    fun.
O Saint Swithun, Saint Swithun," the children cry,
" Why should you christen the apples in mid-July ?

" We don't mind the rain, not an atom.   Away we
    should get
From the schoolroom, bare-headed, bare-footed, out into
    the wet,
If only they'd let us — but that they have never done
    yet ;
And you might as well ask them to — cook us and eat
    us, you see,
For in some things grown-up folk and children can't
    ever agree."

Now hurrah for Saint Swithun !   The rain is o'er ;
Out comes the sun in his glory — they make for the
    door —
Six little feet a-patter, a joyous uproar ;
" Hey ! for Saint Swithun, Saint Swithun," the chil-
    dren shout ;
" Hats and boots — not a moment to lose till we're out."

Hark to the birds and the children! Oh, merry and
    sweet
Rings out the laugh of the children, and quick are
    their feet.
Hey, for the sunshine of summer, its light and its heat!
Where are ye now, little children? Oh, far away,
Though Saint Swithun is christening the apples again
    to-day!

CHILDREN ON THE SHORE.

ANONYMOUS.

We are building little homes on the sands,
    We are making little rooms very gay,
We are busy with our hearts and our hands,
    We are sorry that the time flits away.
Oh, why are the minutes in such haste?
    Oh, why won't they leave us to our play?
Our lessons and our meals are such waste!
    We can dine very well another day.

We do not mind the tide coming in, —
    We can dig it a cunning little bed,
Or leave our pretty house and begin
    Another pretty house in its stead;
We do not mind the sun in our eyes,
    When it makes such a dazzle of the world
That we cannot tell the sea from the skies,
    Nor look where the flying drops are hurl'd.

The shells that we gather are so fair,
　　The birds and the clouds are so kind,
And the wind is so merry with our hair, —
　　It is only the *People* that we mind!
Papa, if you come so very near,
　　We can't build the library to-day;
We think you are tired of being here,
　　And, perhaps, you would like to go away.

There are just one or two we won't refuse,
　　If they come by, to help us now and then;
But we want only friends to be of use,
　　And not all those idle grown-up men;
Perhaps, if we hurry very much,
　　And don't lose an instant of the day,
There'll be time for the last lovely touch
　　Before the sea sweeps it all away.

Oh, children — thus working with the heart!
　　There's nothing so terrible as rest;
Plan only how all may take a part:
　　It's easy for each to do his best.
The sea, sweeping up at set of sun,
　　Can never make your toil be in vain;
It covers the things that you have done,
　　But the joy of the doing shall remain!

———

LITTLE children, love one another.

　　　　　　　　　　　— ST. JOHN IN PATMOS.

THE HAPPIEST LAND.

HENRY W. LONGFELLOW.

THERE sat one day in quiet,
  By an alehouse on the Rhine,
Four hale and hearty fellows,
  And drank the precious wine.

The landlord's daughter filled their cups,
  Around the rustic board;
Then sat they all so calm and still,
  And spake not one rude word.

But, when the maid departed,
  A Swabian raised his hand,
And cried, all hot and flushed with wine,
  "Long live the Swabian land!

"The greatest kingdom upon earth
  Can not with that compare;
With all the stout and hardy men
  And the nut-brown maidens there."

"Ha!" cried a Saxon, laughing,
  And dashed his beard with wine;
"I had rather live in Lapland,
  Than that Swabian land of thine!

"The goodliest land on all this earth
  It is the Saxon land!
There have I as many maidens
  As fingers on this hand!"

"Hold your tongues! both Swabian and Saxon!"
  A bold Bohemian cries:
"If there's a heaven upon this earth
  In Bohemia it lies.

"There the tailor blows the flute,
  And the cobbler blows the horn,
And the miner blows the bugle,
  Over mountain gorge and bourn."

And then the landlord's daughter
  Up to heaven raised her hand,
And said, "Ye may no more contend,
  There lies the happiest land!"

THE CHILD-MUSICIAN.

Austin Dobson.

He had played for his lordship's levee,
  He had played for her ladyship's whim,
Till the poor little head was heavy,
  And the poor little brain would swim.

And the face grew peaked and eerie,
  And the large eyes strange and bright;
And they said — too late — "He is weary!
  He shall rest, for at least to-night!"

But at dawn, when the birds were waking,
  As they watched in the silent room,

With the sound of a strained cord breaking,
  A something snapped in the gloom.

'Twas the string of his violoncello,
  And they heard him stir in his bed: —
"Make room for a tired little fellow,
  Kind God!" was the last he said.

KITTY.

Marion Douglas.

Alas! little Kitty — do give her your pity —
Had lived seven years, and was never called pretty!
  Her hair was bright red and her eyes were dull blue,
    And her cheeks were so freckled,
    They looked like the speckled
  Wild-lilies, which down in the meadow-lands grew.
If her eyes had been black, if she'd only had curls,
She had been, so she thought, the most happy of girls.

Her cousins around her, they pouted and fretted,
But they were all pretty and they were all petted;
  While poor little Kitty, though striving her best
    To do her child's duty,
    Not sharing their beauty,
  Was always neglected and never caressed.
All in vain, so she thought, was she loving and true,
While her hair was bright red, and her eyes were dull
    blue.

But one day, alone 'mid the clover-blooms sitting,
She heard a strange sound, as of wings round her flit-
    ting;
  A light not of sunbeams, a fragrance more sweet
    Than the wind's, blowing over
    The red-blossomed clover,
  Made her thrill with delight from her head to her
    feet;
And a voice, sweet and rare, whispered low in the air,
"See that beautiful, beautiful child sitting there!"

Thrice blessed little Kitty! She almost looked pretty!
Beloved by the angels, she needed no pity!
  O juvenile charmers! with shoulders of snow,
    Ruby lips, sunny tresses, —
    Forms made for caresses, —
  There's one thing, my beauties, 'tis well you should
    know:
Though the world is in love with bright eyes and soft
    hair,
It is only *good* children the angels call fair!

WOODEN LEGS.

POEMS WRITTEN TO A CHILD.

Two children sat in the twilight,
  Murmuring soft and low;
Said one, "I'll be a sailor-lad,
  With my boat ahoy! yo ho!

For sailors are most loved of all
  In every happy home,
And tears of grief or gladness fall
  Just as they go or come."

But the other child said sadly,
  "Ah, do not go to sea,
Or in the dreary winter nights
  What will become of me?
For if the wind began to blow,
  Or thunder shook the sky,
Whilst you were in your boat, yo ho!
  What could I do but cry?"

Then he said, "I'll be a soldier,
  With a delightful gun,
And I'll come home with a wooden leg,
  As heroes have often done."
She screams at that, and prays and begs,
  While tears — half anger — start,
"Don't talk about your wooden legs,
  Unless you'd break my heart!"

He answered her rather proudly,
  "If so, what can I be,
If I must not have a wooden leg
  And must not go to sea?
How could the queen sleep sound at night,
  Safe from the scum and dregs,
If English boys refused to fight
  For fear of wooden legs?"

She hung her head repenting,
   And trying to be good,
But her little hand stroked tenderly
   The leg of flesh and blood!
And with her rosy mouth she kiss'd
   The knickerbocker'd knee,
And sigh'd, "Perhaps — if you insist —
   You'd better go to sea!"

Then he flung his arms about her,
   And laughingly he spoke,
"But I've seen many honest tars
   With legs of British oak!
Oh, darling! when I am a man,
   With beard of shining black,
I'll be a hero if I can,
   And you must not hold me back."

She kissed him as she answered,
   "I'll try what I can do, —
And Wellington had both his legs,
   And Cœur de Lion too!
And Garibaldi," here she sighed,
   "I know he's lame — but there —
He's such a hero — none beside
   Like him could do and dare!"

So the children talked in the twilight
   Of many a setting sun,
And she'd stroke his chin and clap her hands
   That the beard had not begun;

For though she meant to be brave and good
  When he played a hero's part,
Yet often the thought of the wooden leg
  Lay heavy on her heart!

HOW'S MY BOY?

SYDNEY DOBELL.

Ho, sailor of the sea!
How's my boy — my boy?
"What's your boy's name, good wife,
And in what good ship sailed he?"

My boy John —
He that went to sea —
What care I for the ship, sailor?
My boy's my boy to me.

You come back from sea
And not know my John?
I might as well have asked some landsman
Yonder down in the town.
There's not an ass in all the parish
But he knows my John.

How's my boy — my boy?
And unless you let me know
I'll swear you are no sailor,
Blue jacket or no,

Brass button or no, sailor,
Anchor and crown or no!
Sure his ship was the *Jolly Briton* —
"Speak low, woman, speak low!"

And why should I speak low, sailor,
About my own boy John?
If I was loud as I am proud
I'd sing him over the town!
Why should I speak low, sailor?
"That good ship went down."

How's my boy — my boy?
What care I for the ship, sailor,
I never was aboard her.
Be she afloat, or be she aground,
Sinking or swimming, I'll be bound
Her owners can afford her!
I say, how's my John?
"Every man on board went down,
Every man aboard her."

How's my boy — my boy?
What care I for the men, sailor?
I'm not their mother —
How's my boy — my boy?
Tell me of him and no other!
How's my boy — my boy?

LITTLE BELL.

T. B. WESTWOOD.

PIPED the blackbird on the beechwood spray:
" Pretty maid, slow wandering this way,
        What's your name?" quoth he —
" What's your name? Oh, stop and straight unfold,
Pretty maid with showery curls of gold," —
        " Little Bell," said she.

Little Bell sat down beneath the rocks —
Tossed aside her gleaming golden locks —
        " Bonny bird," quoth she,
"Sing me your best song before I go."
" Here's the very finest song I know,
        Little Bell," said he.

And the blackbird piped; you never heard
Half so gay a song from any bird; —
        Full of quips and wiles,
Now so round and rich, now soft and slow,
All for love of that sweet face below,
        Dimpled o'er with smiles.

And the while the bonny bird did pour
His full heart out freely o'er and o'er,
        'Neath the morning skies,
In the little childish heart below,
All the sweetness seemed to grow and grow,
And shine forth in happy overflow
        From the blue, bright eyes.

Down the dell she tripped, and through the glade
Peeped the squirrel from the hazel shade,
    And, from out the tree
Swung, and leaped, and frolicked, void of fear, —
While bold blackbird piped, that all might hear,
    "Little Bell!" piped he.

Little Bell sat down amid the fern:
"Squirrel, squirrel, to your task return —
    Bring me nuts," quoth she.
Up, away the frisky squirrel hies —
Golden wood-lights glancing in his eyes —
    And adown the tree,
Great ripe nuts, kissed brown by July sun,
In the little lap, dropped one by one; —
Hark, how blackbird pipes to see the fun!
    "Happy Bell!" pipes he.

Little Bell looked up and down the glade; —
"Squirrel, squirrel, if you're not afraid,
    Come and share with me!"
Down came squirrel, eager for his fare, —
Down came bonny blackbird, I declare!
Little Bell gave each his honest share;
    Ah, the merry three!

And the while these frolic playmates twain
Piped and frisked from bough to bough again,
    'Neath the morning skies,
In the little childish heart below,
All the sweetness seemed to grow and grow,

And shine out in happy overflow,
   From her blue, bright eyes.

By her snow-white cot at close of day,
Knelt sweet Bell, with folded palms to pray:
   Very calm and clear
Rose the praying voice to where, unseen,
In blue heaven, an angel shape serene
   Paused awhile to hear.

"What good child is this," the angel said,
"That, with happy heart, beside her bed
   Prays so lovingly?"
Low and soft, oh! very low and soft,
Crooned the blackbird in the orchard croft,
   "Bell, *dear* Bell!" crooned he.

"Whom God's creatures love," the angel fair
Murmured, "God doth bless with angels' care;
   Child, thy bed shall be
Folded safe from harm. Love, deep and kind,
Shall watch around, and leave good gifts behind,
   Little Bell, for thee."

PRAYING AND LOVING.

S. T. COLERIDGE. FROM "THE ANCIENT MARINER."

HE prayeth best who loveth best
   All things, both great and small,
For the dear God who loveth us,
   He made and loveth all.

THE ANGEL'S WHISPER.

SAMUEL LOVER.

A BABY was sleeping;
Its mother was weeping;
For her husband was far on the wild raging sea;
And the tempest was swelling
Round the fisherman's dwelling,
And she cried, "Dermot, darling, Oh, come back to me!"

Her beads while she numbered
The baby still slumbered,
And smiled in her face as she bended her knee.
"Oh, blest be that warning,
That sweet sleep adorning,
For I know that the angels are whispering to thee!

"And while they are keeping
Bright watch o'er thy sleeping,
Oh, pray to them softly, my baby, with me!
And say thou wouldst rather
They'd watch o'er thy father,
For I know that the angels are whispering to thee."

The dawn of the morning
Saw Dermot returning,
And the wife wept with joy her babe's father to see;
And closely caressing
Her child with a blessing,
Said, "I knew that the angels were whispering with
        thee."

THE LITTLE NURSE.

FROM THE FRENCH OF MME. TASTU.   TRANSLATED AND ARRANGED BY THE EDITORS.

My mother has but just gone out;
  She'll come back soon, she said,
And bade me stay till then about,
  To watch your curly head.
Indeed I wish that she were here;
  Why won't you smile, oh, why?
Don't cry, my little brother dear;
  O baby, don't you cry!

What is there that you'd like of mine?
  Look, see the carriage come!
Or shall I knock the window pane
  And beat it like a drum?
Oh, dear! will nothing make you good?
  Stop quick, or I shall fly!
Don't cry, my little brother dear,
  O baby, please don't cry!

I know a story, nice and long;
  I'll tell it if you will! —
I know a lovely, lovely song;
  I'll sing if you'll be still!
No; nothing yet but scream and tear:
  Oh, fie upon you, fie!
Don't cry, my little brother dear;
  O baby, don't you cry!

You naughty, naughty little child!
  Alas! what shall I do?
I'll pray to Holy Mary mild,
  She had a baby too —
Oh, joy! here comes our mother!
  Oh, how relieved am I!
Don't cry, dear little brother,
  Please, baby, don't you cry!

THE COMMON QUESTION.

JOHN G. WHITTIER.

BEHIND us at our evening meal
  The gray bird ate his fill,
Swung downward by a single claw,
  And wiped his hookèd bill.

He shook his wings and crimson tail
  And set his head aslant,
And, in his sharp, impatient way,
  Asked, "What does Charlie want?"

"Fie, silly bird!" I answered, "tuck
  Your head beneath your wing,
And go to sleep"; — but o'er and o'er
  He asked the self-same thing.

Then, smiling, to myself I said: —
  How like are men and birds!
We all are saying what he says,
  In action and in words.

The boy with whip and top and drum,
    The girl with hoop and doll,
And men with lands and houses, ask
    The question of poor Poll.

However full, with something more
    We fain the bag would cram;
We sigh above our crowded nets
    For fish that never swam.

No bounty of indulgent Heaven
    The vague desire can stay;
Self-love is still a Tartar mill,
    For grinding prayers alway.

The dear God hears and pities all,
    He knoweth all our wants;
And what we blindly ask of Him,
    His love withholds or grants.

And so I sometimes think our prayers
    Might well be merged in one;
And nest and perch, and hearth and church,
    Repeat, "Thy will be done!"

A LITTLE GOOSE.

Eliza Sproat Turner.

THE chill November day was done,
    The working world home faring;
The wind came whistling through the streets
    And set the gas-lamps flaring;

And hopelessly and aimlessly
   The scared old leaves were flying,
When, mingled with the sighing wind,
   I heard a small voice crying.

And shivering on the corner stood
   A child of four or over;
No cloak nor hat her small soft arms
   And wind-blown curls to cover.
Her dimpled face was stained with tears;
   Her round blue eyes ran over;
She cherished in her wee, cold hand
   A bunch of faded clover.

And, one hand round her treasure, while
   She slipped in mine the other,
Half-scared, half-confidential, said,
   "Oh, please, I want my mother!"
"Tell me your street and number, pet;
   Don't cry, I'll take you to it."
Sobbing, she answered, "I forget —
   The organ made me do it.

"He came and played at Milly's steps,
   The monkey took the money,
And so I followed down the street,
   The monkey was so funny!
I've walked about a hundred hours,
   From one street to another;
The monkey's gone, I've spoiled my flowers;
   Oh, please, I want my mother!"

"But, what's your mother's name, and what
  The street? Now think a minute."
"My mother's name is 'Mamma dear';
  The street — I can't begin it."
"But what is strange about the house,
  Or new, not like the others?"
"I guess you mean my trundle-bed,
  Mine and my little brother's.

"Oh, dear! I ought to be at home,
  To help him say his prayers,
He's such a baby, he forgets,
  And we are both such players —
And there's a bar between, to keep
  From pitching on each other,
For Harry rolls when he's asleep.
  Oh, dear! I want my mother."

The sky grew stormy; people passed
  All muffled, homeward faring;
"You'll have to spend the night with me,"
  I said at last, despairing.
I tied a kerchief round her neck —
  "What ribbon's this, my blossom?"
"Why, don't you know?" she smiling asked,
  And drew it from her bosom.

A card with number, street, and name!
  My eyes astonished met it;
"For," said the little one, "you see
  I might sometime forget it;

And so I wear a little thing,
That tells you all about it;
For mother says she's very sure
I would get lost without it."

ABOU BEN ADHEM.

LEIGH HUNT.

ABOU BEN ADHEM (may his tribe increase!)
Awoke one night from a deep dream of peace,
And saw within the moonlight of his room,
Making it rich, and like a lily in bloom,
An angel writing in a book of gold.
Exceeding peace had made Ben Adhem bold,
And, to the presence in the room, he said,
"What writest thou?"   The vision raised its head,
And, with a look made of all sweet accord,
Answered, "The names of those who love the Lord!"
"And is mine one?" asked Abou. — "Nay, not so,"
Replied the angel.   Abou spake more low,
But cheerly still; and said — "I pray thee, then,
Write me as one that loves his fellow-men."
The angel wrote and vanished.   The next night
It came again, with a great wakening light,
And showed the names whom love of God had blest;
And lo! Ben Adhem's name led all the rest!

THE PARROT.

Thomas Campbell.

A PARROT, from the Spanish main,
   Full young and early caged came o'er,
With bright wings, to the bleak domain
    Of Mulla's shore.

To spicy groves where he had won
   His plumage of resplendent hue,
His native fruits, and skies, and sun,
    He bade adieu.

For these he changed the smoke of turf,
   A heathery land and misty sky,
And turned on rocks and raging surf
    His golden eye.

But petted in our climate cold,
   He lived and chattered many a day:
Until with age, from green and gold
    His wings grew gray.

At last when blind, and seeming dumb,
   He scolded, laugh'd, and spoke no more,
A Spanish stranger chanced to come
    To Mulla's shore.

He hailed the bird in Spanish speech,
   The bird in Spanish speech replied;
Flapped round the cage with joyous screech,
    Dropt down, and died.

WE ARE SEVEN.

WILLIAM WORDSWORTH.

I MET a little cottage girl:
　　She was eight years old, she said;
Her hair was thick with many a curl
　　That clustered round her head.

She had a rustic, woodland air,
　　And she was wildly clad;
Her eyes were fair, and very fair; —
　　Her beauty made me glad.

"Sisters and brothers, little maid,
　　How many may you be?"
"How many? Seven in all," she said,
　　And wondering looked at me.

"And where are they? I pray you tell."
　　She answered, "Seven are we;
And two of us at Conway dwell,
　　And two are gone to sea.

"Two of us in the churchyard lie,
　　My sister and my brother;
And in the churchyard cottage, I
　　Dwell near them with my mother."

"You say that two at Conway dwell,
　　And two are gone to sea,
Yet ye are seven! I pray you tell,
　　Sweet maid, how this may be?"

Then did the little maid reply,
  " Seven boys and girls are we;
Two of us in the churchyard lie,
  Beneath the churchyard tree."

" You run about, my little maid;
  Your limbs they are alive;
If two are in the churchyard laid,
  Then ye are only five."

" Their graves are green, they may be seen,"
  The little maid replied,
" Twelve steps or more from mother's door,
  And they are side by side.

" My stockings there I often knit,
  My kerchief there I hem;
And there upon the ground I sit,
  And sing a song to them.

" And often after sunset, sir,
  When it is light and fair,
I take my little porringer,
  And eat my supper there.

" The first that died was sister Jane;
  In bed she moaning lay,
Till God released her from her pain;
  And then she went away.

" So in the churchyard she was laid;
  And, when the grass was dry,

Together round her grave we played,
  My brother John and I.

"And when the ground was white with snow,
  And I could run and slide,
My brother John was forced to go,
  And he lies by her side."

"How many are you, then," said I,
  "If they two are in heaven?"
Quick was the little maid's reply,
  "O Master! we are seven."

"But they are dead; those two are dead;
  Their spirits are in heaven!"
'Twas throwing words away; for still
The little maid would have her will;
  And said, "Nay, we are seven."

WHICH SHALL IT BE?

Anonymous.

"Which shall it be? Which shall it be?"
I looked at John, John looked at me;
And when I found that I must speak,
My voice seemed strangely low and weak.
"Tell me again what Robert said;"
And then I, listening, bent my head —
This is his letter: "I will give
A house and land while you shall live,

If in return from out your seven
One child to me for aye is given."

I looked at John's old garments worn;
I thought of all that he had borne
Of poverty, and work, and care,
Which I, though willing, could not share;
I thought of seven young mouths to feed,
Of seven little children's need,
   And then of this.

   "Come, John," said I,
"We'll choose among them as they lie
Asleep." So, walking hand in hand,
Dear John and I surveyed our band:
First to the cradle lightly stepped,
Where Lilian, the baby, slept.
Softly the father stooped to lay
His rough hand down in loving way,
When dream or whisper made her stir,
And huskily he said: "Not her!"

We stooped beside the trundle bed,
And one long ray of lamplight shed
Athwart the boyish faces there,
In sleep so pitiful and fair;
I saw on Jamie's rough, red cheek
A tear undried. Ere John could speak,
"He's but a baby too," said I,
And kissed him as we hurried by.
Pale, patient Robbie's angel face

Still in his sleep bore suffering's trace —
"No, for a thousand crowns, not him!"
He whispered, while our eyes were dim.

Poor Dick! bad Dick! our wayward son —
Turbulent, restless, idle one —
Could he be spared? Nay, He who gave
Bade us befriend him to the grave;
Only a mother's heart could be
Patient enough for such as he;
"And so," said John, "I would not dare
To take him from her bedside prayer."

Then stole we softly up above,
And knelt by Mary, child of love;
"Perhaps for her 'twould better be,"
I said to John. Quite silently
He lifted up a curl that lay
Across her cheek in wilful way,
And shook his head: "Nay, love, not thee,"
The while my heart beat audibly.

Only one more, our eldest lad,
Trusty and truthful, good and glad,
So like his father. "No, John, no!
I cannot, will not, let him go."
And so we wrote in courteous way,
We could not give one child away;
And afterwards toil lighter seemed,
Thinking of that of which we dreamed,
Happy in truth that not one face

Was missed from its accustomed place;
Thankful to work for all the seven,
Trusting the rest to One in Heaven!

THE PET LAMB.

WILLIAM WORDSWORTH.

THE dew was falling fast, the stars began to blink;
I heard a voice; it said, "Drink, pretty creature, drink!"
And, looking o'er the hedge, before me I espied
A snow-white mountain-lamb, with a maiden at its side.

Nor sheep nor kine were near; the lamb was all alone,
And by a slender cord was tethered to a stone.
With one knee on the grass did the little maiden kneel,
While to that mountain-lamb she gave its evening meal.

The lamb, while from her hand he thus his supper took,
Seemed to feast with head and ears, and his tail with
        pleasure shook.
"Drink, pretty creature, drink!" she said, in such a tone
That I almost received her heart into my own.

'Twas little Barbara Lewthwaite, a child of beauty rare!
I watched them with delight; they were a lovely pair.
Now with her empty can the maiden turned away,
But ere ten yards were gone her footsteps did she stay.

Right toward the lamb she looked; and from a shady
        place,
I, unobserved, could see the workings of her face.

" If nature to her tongue could measured numbers bring,
Thus," thought I, " to her lamb that little maid might
    sing : —

" What ails thee, young one ? what ?   Why pull so at
    thy cord ?
Is it not well with thee ? well both for bed and board ?
Thy plot of grass is soft, and green as grass can be ;
Rest, little young one, rest ; what is't that aileth thee ?

" What is it thou would'st seek ?   What is wanting to
    thy heart ?
Thy limbs, are they not strong ? and beautiful thou art.
This grass is tender grass, these flowers have no peers,
And that green corn all day is rustling in thy ears.

" If the sun be shining hot, do but stretch thy woollen
    chain, —
This beech is standing by, — its covert thou canst gain.
For rain and mountain storms, the like thou needst not
    fear ;
The rain and storm are things that scarcely can come
    here.

" Rest, little young one, rest ; thou hast forgot the day
When my father found thee first, in places far away.
Many flocks were on the hills, but thou wert owned by
    none,
And thy mother from thy side forevermore was gone.

" He took thee in his arms, and in pity brought thee
    home, —

A blessed day for thee ! — then whither would'st thou
    roam ?
A faithful nurse thou hast ; the dam that did thee yean
Upon the mountain-tops no kinder could have been.

" Thou know'st that twice a day I have brought thee
    in this can
Fresh water from the brook, as clear as ever ran ;
And twice in the day, when the ground is wet with dew,
I bring thee draughts of milk, — warm milk it is, and
    new.

" Thy limbs will shortly be twice as stout as they are
    now ;
Then I'll yoke thee to my cart, like a pony to the plough.
My playmate thou shalt be, and when the wind is cold,
Our hearth shall be thy bed, our house shall be thy fold.

" It will not, will not rest !   Poor creature, can it be
That 'tis thy mother's heart which is working so in
    thee ?
Things that I know not of belike to thee are dear,
And dreams of things which thou canst neither see nor
    hear.

" Alas, the mountain-tops that look so green and fair !
I've heard of fearful winds and darkness that come
    there.
The little brooks, that seem all pastime and all play,
When they are angry roar like lions for their prey.

" Here thou need'st not dread the raven in the sky ;

Night and day thou art safe — our cottage is hard by.
Why bleat so after me ? why pull so at thy chain ?
Sleep, — and at break of day I will come to thee again !"

As homeward through the lane I went with lazy feet,
This song to myself did I oftentimes repeat ;
And it seemed, as I retraced the ballad line by line,
That but half of it was hers and one half of it was mine.

Again and once again did I repeat the song:
"Nay," said I, "more than half to the damsel must
     belong;
For she looked with such a look, and she spake with
     such a tone,
That I almost received her heart into my own."

THE DEATH OF LITTLE NELL.

CHARLES DICKENS. FROM "THE OLD CURIOSITY SHOP."

SHE was dead. There upon her little bed, she lay at
rest. The solemn stillness was no marvel now. She
was dead. No sleep so beautiful and calm, so free from
trace of pain, so fair to look upon. She seemed a creature fresh from the hand of God, and waiting for the
breath of life ; not one who had lived and suffered
death. Her couch was dressed with here and there
some winter berries and green leaves gathered in a spot
she had been used to favor. "When I die, put near me
something that had loved the light and had the sky
above it always." Those were her words.

She was dead. Dear, gentle, patient, noble Nell was dead. Her little bird — a poor, slight thing the pressure of a finger would have crushed — was stirring nimbly in its cage; and the strong heart of its child mistress was mute and motionless forever.

A TURKISH LEGEND.

T. B. ALDRICH.

A CERTAIN pasha, dead five thousand years,
Once from his harem fled in sudden tears,

And had this sentence on the city's gate
Deeply engraven, "Only God is great."

So these four words above the city's noise
Hung like the accents of an angel's voice.

And evermore from the high barbacan,
Saluted each returning caravan.

Lost is that city's glory. Every gust
Lifts, with crisp leaves, the unknown pasha's dust,

And all is ruin, save one wrinkled gate
Whereon is written, "Only God is great."

THE WORLD.

FRIEDRICH SCHILLER. TRANSLATION OF E. L. BULWER.

THERE is a mansion vast and fair,
That doth on unseen pillars rest;

No wanderer leaves the portals there,
Yet each how brief a guest!
The craft by which that mansion rose
No thought can picture to the soul;
'Tis lighted by a lamp which throws
Its stately shimmer through the whole,
As crystal clear it rears aloof
The single gem that forms its roof:
And never hath the eye surveyed
The Master who that mansion made.

CONTENT AND DISCONTENT.

RICHARD C. TRENCH.

SOME murmur, when their sky is clear
And wholly bright to view,
If one small speck of dark appear
In their great heaven of blue;
And some with thankful love are filled,
If but one streak of light,
One ray of God's good mercy, gild
The darkness of their night.

TO–DAY.

THOMAS CARLYLE.

So here hath been dawning
Another blue day:

Think wilt thou let it
　　Slip useless away.

Out of Eternity
　　This new day is born;
Into Eternity,
　　At night, will return.

Behold it aforetime
　　No eye ever did;
So soon it forever
　　From all eyes is hid.

Here hath been dawning
　　Another blue day;
Think wilt thou let it
　　Slip useless away.

A CHILD'S THOUGHT OF GOD.

ELIZABETH BARRETT BROWNING.

THEY say that God lives very high,
　　But if you look above the pines
You cannot see our God; and why?

And if you dig down in the mines,
　　You never see him in the gold;
Though from him all that glory shines.

God is so good, he wears a fold
　　Of heaven and earth across his face —
Like secrets kept, for love, untold.

But still I feel that his embrace
　Slides down by thrills, through all things made,
Through sight and sound of every place;

As if my tender mother laid
　On my shut lids her tender pressure,
Half-waking me at night, and said,
　"Who kissed you in the dark, dear guesser?"

THE HEAVENLY DOVE.

FREDERIKA BREMER. TRANSLATION OF MARY HOWITT.

THERE sitteth a dove, so white and fair,
　All on the lily spray,
And she listeth how to Jesus Christ
　The little children pray.

Lightly she spreads her friendly wings,
　And to Heaven's gate hath sped,
And unto the Father in Heaven she bears
　The prayers which the children have said.

And back she comes from Heaven's gate;
　And brings — that Dove so mild —
From the Father in Heaven, who hears her speak,
　A blessing for every child.

Then, children, lift up a pious prayer;
　It hears whatever you say —
That Heavenly Dove, so white and fair,
　That sits on the lily spray.

HUMILITY.

ROBERT HERRICK.

HUMBLE we must be
If to Heaven we go.
High is the roof there,
But the gate is low.

WINNING AND LOSING.

DINAH MARIA MULOCK.

"PEACE on earth and mercy mild,"
Sing the angels, reconciled,
Over each sad warfare done,
Each soul-battle lost and won.

He that has a victory lost,
May discomfit yet a host;
And, it often doth befall,
He who conquers loses all.

FAULTS AND VIRTUES.

JOHN RUSKIN.

Do not think of your faults; still less of others'
faults; in every person who comes near you, look for
what is good and strong; honor that; rejoice in it;
and, as you can, try to imitate it; and your faults will
drop off like dead leaves, when their time comes.

GOOD NAME.

William Shakespeare.

Good name in man and woman, dear my lord,
Is the immediate jewel of their souls:
Who steals my purse, steals trash; 'tis something,
    nothing;
'Twas mine, 'tis his, and has been slave to thousands;
But he that filches from me my good name,
Robs me of that which not enriches him,
And makes me poor indeed.

THE MOON.

Anonymous.

O Moon, said the children, O Moon, that shineth fair,
Why do you stay so far away, so high above us there?
O Moon, you must be very cold from shining on the
    sea;
If you would come and play with us, how happy we
    should be!

O children, said the Moon, I shine above your head,
That I may light the ships at night, when the sun
    has gone to bed;
That I may show the beggar-boy his way across the
    moor,
And bring the busy farmer home to his own cottage-
    door.

O Moon, said the children, may we shine in your
    place ?
They say that I have sunny hair, and I a sparkling
    face.
To light the ships and beggar-boys we greatly do
    desire;
And you might come and warm yourself before the
    nursery fire!

O children, said the Moon, we have each allotted
    parts:
'Tis yours to shine by love divine on happy human
    hearts;
'Tis mine to make the pathway bright of wanderers
    that roam;
'Tis yours to scatter endless light on those that stay
    at home!

GOD THE FATHER.

H. W. BEECHER.

THE sun does not shine for a few trees and flowers,
but for the wide world's joy. The lonely pine on
the mountain-top waves its sombre boughs, and cries,
"Thou art my sun!" And the little meadow-violet
lifts its cup of blue, and whispers with its perfumed
breath, "Thou art my sun!" And the grain in a
thousand fields rustles in the wind, and makes answer,
"Thou art my sun!"

So God sits effulgent in Heaven, not for a favored

few, but for the universe of life; and there is no creature so poor or so low that he may not look up with
childlike confidence, and say, "My Father! thou art
mine!"

HAPPINESS.

JOHN KEBLE.

THERE are, in this rude stunning tide
  Of human care and crime;
With whom the melodies abide
  Of the everlasting chime;
Who carry music in their heart,
Through dusty lane and wrangling mart,
Plying their daily toil with busier feet,
Because their secret souls a holy strain repeat.

SPEAK GENTLY.

ANONYMOUS.

SPEAK gently; it is better far
  To rule by love than fear;
Speak gently; let no harsh word mar
  The good we may do here.
Speak gently to the little child;
  Its love be sure to gain;
Teach it in accents soft and mild;
  It may not long remain.

Speak gently to the young; for they
  Will have enough to bear;
Pass through this life as best they may,
  'Tis full of anxious care.
Speak gently to the aged one,
  Grieve not the care-worn heart,
Whose sands of life are nearly run;
  Let such in peace depart.

Speak gently to the erring; know
  They must have toiled in vain;
Perchance unkindness made them so;
  Oh, win them back again.
Speak gently; 'tis a little thing
  Dropped in the heart's deep well;
The good, the joy, that it may bring,
  Eternity shall tell.

ONE BY ONE.

Adelaide A. Procter.

ONE by one the sands are flowing,
  One by one the moments fall;
Some are coming, some are going;
  Do not strive to grasp them all.

One by one thy duties wait thee —
  Let thy whole strength go to each,
Let no future dreams elate thee,
  Learn thou first what these can teach.

One by one (bright gifts from heaven)
   Joys are sent thee here below;
Take them readily when given —
   Ready, too, to let them go.

One by one thy griefs shall meet thee;
   Do not fear an armèd band;
One will fade as others greet thee —
   Shadows passing through the land.

Do not look at life's long sorrow;
   See how small each moment's pain;
God will help thee for to-morrow,
   So each day begin again.

Every hour that fleets so slowly
   Has its task to do or bear;
Luminous the crown, and holy,
   When each gem is set with care.

Do not linger with regretting,
   Or for passing hours despond;
Nor, thy daily toil forgetting,
   Look too eagerly beyond.

Hours are golden links, God's token,
   Reaching heaven; but, one by one,
Take them, lest the chain be broken
   Ere the pilgrimage be done.

DUTY.

R. W. EMERSON.

So nigh is grandeur to our dust,
  So near is God to man,
When Duty whispers low, " *Thou must*,"
  The youth replies, " *I can*."

TIME.

BENJAMIN FRANKLIN.

IF Time be of all things the most precious, wasting
Time must be the greatest prodigality, since lost Time
is never found again; and what we call Time enough,
always proves little enough. Let us then be up and
doing to the purpose; so by diligence shall we so move
with less perplexity. Sloth makes all things difficult;
but Industry, all easy. He that riseth late must trot
all day, and shall scarce overtake his business at night;
while Laziness travels so slowly that Poverty soon over-
takes him. Drive thy business; let not that drive
thee: and early to bed and early to rise, makes a man
healthy, and wealthy, and wise.

HE who has a thousand friends has not a friend to
    spare,
And he who has one enemy shall meet him everywhere.

CONSIDER.

CHRISTINA G. ROSSETTI.

CONSIDER
The lilies of the field, whose bloom is brief —
   We are as they;
   Like them we fade away,
     As doth a leaf.

Consider
The sparrows of the air, of small account:
   Our God doth view
   Whether they fall or mount —
     He guards us too.

Consider
The lilies, that do neither spin nor toil,
   Yet are most fair —
   What profits all this care,
     And all this coil?

Consider
The birds, that have no barn nor harvest-weeks;
   God gives them food —
   Much more our Father seeks
     To do us good.

GOODNESS.

MARCUS AURELIUS.

WHATEVER any one does or says, I must be good; just as if the gold, or the emerald, or the purple were always saying this, "Whatever any one else does, I must be emerald and keep my color."

TO MY SOUL.

PAUL FLEMING. TRANSLATED BY THE EDITORS.

GRIEVE not with sighing
And crying, —
    Be still.
God is thy guide,
Be satisfied,
    My will!

What thou to-day would'st borrow,
To-morrow,
    The One
Who stands for all,
Shall in thy hands let fall,
    Thine own.

Under Fate's fiat
Rest quiet;
    Stand fast!
Whate'er God will
Of good or ill
    Is best.

THE NOBLE NATURE.

BEN JONSON.

IT is not growing like a tree
In bulk, doth make men better be;
Or standing long an oak three hundred year,
To fall a log at last, dry, bald, and sere;
    A lily of a day
    Is fairer far in May,
Although it fall and die that night;
It was the plant and flower of Light.
In small proportions we just beauty see;
And in short measures life may perfect be.

A WISH.

BEN JONSON.

THE fairy beam upon you,
The stars to glister on you;
    A moon of light
    In the noon of night,
Till the fire drake hath o'ergone you!
The wheel of fortune guide you,
The boy with the bow beside you
    Run aye in the way,
    Till the bird of day
And the luckier lot betide you!

MARTIN LUTHER'S LETTER TO HIS LITTLE SON.

ARRANGED. ANONYMOUS TRANSLATION.

GRACE and peace in Christ, my darling little son: I am glad to see that you study and pray diligently. Go on doing so, my Johnny, and when I come home I will bring some fine things for you. I know of a beautiful, pleasant garden where many children go, and have little golden coats, and gather from the trees fine apples, and pears, and cherries and plums; they sing and play, and are happy; they have beautiful little horses with golden bits and silver saddles. I asked the owner of the garden, whose children these were. He replied, "They are children that love to pray and to learn, and are good." I then said, "Dear sir, I, too, have a son, whose name is Johnny Luther. May he not also come into the garden, that he, too, may eat these beautiful apples and pears, and ride on these fine horses, and play with the boys?" The man said, "If he loves to pray and to learn, and is good, he shall come into the garden." And he showed me a fine grass plot in the garden for dancing, and there were hanging nothing but golden fifes and drums and fine silver crossbows. But it was early, and the children had not yet dined; and as I could not wait for their dancing, I said to the man, "O my dear sir, I will hasten away, and write all about this to my dear little Johnny, that he may pray and learn diligently and be good, and then come into this garden." And now I commend you to God.

Your dear father, MARTIN LUTHER.

THREE PAIRS AND ONE.

CLEMENT L. SMITH. FROM THE GERMAN OF FRIEDRICH RÜCKERT.

EARS thou hast two and mouth but one:
　　The intent dost seek?
Thou art to listen much, it means,
　　And little speak.

Eyes thou hast two and mouth but one:
　　Is the mystery deep?
Much thou shalt see, it means, or much
　　Thy silence keep.

Hands thou hast two and mouth but one:
　　" Why?" dost repeat?
The two are there to labor with,
　　The one to eat.

THE TONGUE.

JOHN LYLY. "EUPHUES."

WE may see the cunning and curious work of nature, which hath barred and hedged nothing in, so
strongly as the tongue, with two rows of teeth, and
therewith two lips. Besides she hath placed it far
from the hearte that it shoulde not utter that which
the hearte had conceived; this also shoulde cause us
to be silent, seeing those that use muche talke,
though they speake truely are never believed.

I–HAVE AND OH! HAD–I.

TRANSLATION ANONYMOUS. FROM THE GERMAN OF LANGHEIM.

THERE are two little songsters well known in the land,
  Their names are "I-have" and "Oh! had-I,"
"I-have" will come tamely and perch on your hand,
  But "Oh! had-I" will mock you most sadly.

This bird is at first far less fair to the eye,
  But his worth is by far more enduring
Than a thousand "Oh! had-I's" that sit far and high
  On roofs and on trees so alluring.

Full many a golden egg this bird will lay,
  And sing you, "Be cheery! Be cheery!"
While merry your life shall be all the long day,
  And sweet shall your sleep be when weary.

But let an "Oh! had-I" but once take your eye,
  And a longing to catch him once seize you,
He'll give you no comfort nor rest till you die,
  Life long he'll torment you and tease you.

He'll keep you all day running up and down hill,
  Now racing and panting, now creeping,
While far overhead the sweet bird at his will,
  With his bright, golden plumage is sweeping.

Now every wise man who attends to my song,
  Will count his "I-have" a choice treasure,
And if e'er an "Oh! had-I" comes flying along,
  Will just let him fly at his pleasure.

LITTLE BROWN HANDS.

M. H. Krout.

They drive home the cows from the pasture,
　Up through the long shady lane,
Where the quail whistles loud in the wheat-fields,
　That are yellow with ripening grain.
They find in the thick waving grasses,
　Where the scarlet-lipped strawberry grows.
They gather the earliest snowdrops,
　And the first crimson buds of the rose.

They toss the new hay in the meadow;
　They gather the elder-bloom white;
They find where the dusky grapes purple
　In the soft-tinted October light.
They know where the apples hang ripest,
　And are sweeter than Italy's wines;
They know where the fruit hangs the thickest
　On the long, thorny blackberry-vines.

They gather the delicate sea-weeds,
　And build tiny castles of sand;
They pick up the beautiful sea-shells, —
　Fairy barks that have drifted to land.
They wave from the tall, rocking tree-tops
　Where the oriole's hammock-nest swings;
And at night-time are folded in slumber
　By a song that a fond mother sings.

Those who toil bravely are strongest;
　The humble and poor become great;

And so from these brown-handed children
   Shall grow mighty rulers of state.
The pen of the author and statesman, —
   The noble and wise of the land, —
The sword, and the chisel, and palette,
   Shall be held in the little brown hand.

OVER AND OVER AGAIN.

Anonymous.

Over and over again,
   No matter which way I turn,
I always find in the book of life,
   Some lesson I have to learn.
I must take my turn at the mill,
   I must grind out the golden grain,
I must work at my task with a resolute will,
   Over and over again.

We cannot measure the need
   Of even the tiniest flower,
Nor check the flow of the golden sands
   That run through a single hour ;
But the morning dews must fall,
   And the sun and the summer rain
Must do their part, and perform it all
   Over and over again.

Over and over again
   The brook through the meadows flows,

And over and over again
  The ponderous mill-wheel goes.
Once doing will not suffice,
  Though doing be not in vain;
And a blessing failing us once or twice,
  May come if we try again.

The path that has once been trod,
  Is never so rough to the feet;
And the lesson we once have learned,
  Is never so hard to repeat.
Though sorrowful tears must fall,
  And the heart to its depths be driven
With storm and tempest, we need them all
  To render us meet for Heaven.

SUNSHINE.

FROM THE FRENCH OF DELAVIGNE.   TRANSLATED AND ARRANGED BY THE EDITORS.

WHEN the bright sun
  Doth smiling rise,
A ruddy ball
  Through cloudy skies,

The wood and field
To him do yield,
And flower and leaf
Forget their grief.

In childish hearts
  So springs delight,

Chasing black care
Back into night.

Joys, like the flowers,
In children rise;
They smile with tears
Still in their eyes.

SIXTY AND SIX.

Thomas Wentworth Higginson. "Fons Delicium Domus."

Joy of the morning,
Darling of dawning,
Blithe little, lithe little daughter of mine,
While with thee ranging,
Sure I'm exchanging
Sixty of my years for six years like thine.
Wings cannot vie with thee,
Lightly I fly with thee,
Gay as the thistle-down over the lea;
Life is all magic,
Comic or tragic,
Played as thou playest it daily with me.

Floating and ringing,
Thy merry singing
Comes when the light comes, like that of the birds.
List to the play of it, —
That is the way of it;
All's in the music and naught in the words.

Glad or grief-laden,
　　Schubert or Haydn,
Ballad of Erin, or merry Scotch lay;
　　Like an evangel,
　　Some baby angel,
Brought from sky-nursery, stealing away.

　　Surely I know it,
　　Artist nor poet
Guesses my treasure of jubilant hours.
　　Sorrows, what are they?
　　Nearer or far, they
Vanish in sunshine, like dew from the flowers.
　　Years, I am glad of them!
　　Would that I had of them
More and yet more, while thus mingled with thine.
　　Age, I make light of it,
　　Fear not the sight of it;
Time's but our playmate, whose toys are divine.

SEVEN TIMES ONE.

JEAN INGELOW.

THERE's no dew left on the daisies and clover,
　　There's no rain left in heaven;
I've said my "seven times" over and over,
　　Seven times one are seven.

I am old, so old I can write a letter;
　　My birthday lessons are done;

The lambs play always, they know no better, —
    They are only one times one.

O Moon! in the night I have seen you sailing
    And shining so round and low;
You were bright, ah bright! but your light is failing, —
    You are nothing now but a bow.

You Moon, have you done something wrong in heaven,
    That God has hidden your face?
I hope if you have, you will soon be forgiven,
    And shine again in your place.

O velvet bee, you're a dusty fellow;
    You've powdered your legs with gold!
O brave marshmary buds, rich and yellow,
    Give me your money to hold!

O columbine, open your folded wrapper,
    Where two twin turtle-doves dwell!
O cuckoo-pint, toll me the purple clapper
    That hangs in your clear green bell!

And show me your nest, with the young ones in it, —
    I will not steal it away;
I am old! you may trust me, linnet, linnet, —
    I am seven times one to-day.

LITTLE things
On little wings
Bear little souls to Heaven.

MY LITTLE LADY.

T. B. WESTWOOD.

THE queen is proud on her throne,
 And proud are her maids so fine;
But the proudest lady that ever was known
 Is this little lady of mine.
And oh! she flouts me, she flouts me!
And spurns, and scorns, and scouts me!
Though I drop on my knees, and sue for grace,
And beg and beseech with the saddest face,
 Still ever the same she doubts me.

She is seven by the calendar,
 A lily's almost as tall;
But oh! this little lady's by far
 The proudest lady of all!
It's her sport and pleasure to flout me!
To spurn and scorn and scout me!
But ah! I've a notion it's naught but play,
And that, say what she will and feign what she may,
 She can't well do without me!

For at times, like a pleasant tune,
 A sweeter mood o'ertakes her;
Oh! then she's sunny as skies of June,
 And all her pride forsakes her.
Oh! she dances around me so fairly!
Oh! her laugh rings out so rarely!
Oh! she coaxes, and nestles, and peers, and pries,
In my puzzled face with her two great eyes,
 And owns she loves me dearly.

THE SCULPTOR.

GEORGE WASHINGTON DOANE.

CHISEL in hand stood the sculptor-boy,
    With his marble block before him ;
And his face lit up with a smile of joy
    As an angel-dream passed o'er him :
He carved the dream on that shapeless stone
    With many a sharp incision ;
With Heaven's own light the sculpture shone :
    He had caught that angel-vision.

Sculptors of life are we as we stand
    With our souls uncarved before us,
Waiting the hour when at God's command
    Our life-dream shall pass o'er us.
If we carve it then on the yielding stone
    With many a sharp incision,
Its heavenly beauty shall be our own,
    Our lives that angel-vision.

CHILD AND MOTHER.

THOMAS HOOD.

LOVE thy mother, little one !
Kiss and clasp her neck again !
Hereafter she may have a son
Will kiss and clasp her neck in vain.
    Love thy mother, little one !

Gaze upon her living eyes,
And mirror back her love for thee!
Hereafter thou may'st shudder sighs
To meet them when they cannot see.
    Gaze upon her living eyes!

Press her lips, the while they glow
With love that they have often told!
Hereafter thou may'st press in woe,
And kiss them till thine own are cold.
    Press her lips, the while they glow!

Oh, revere her raven hair, —
Although it be not silver gray!
Too early, Death, led on by care,
May snatch, save one dear lock, away.
    Oh, revere her raven hair!

Pray for her at eve and morn,
That Heaven may long the stroke defer;
For thou may'st live the hour forlorn,
When thou wilt ask to die with her.
    Pray for her at eve and morn!

MOTHER, WATCH!

ANONYMOUS.

MOTHER, watch the little feet
    Climbing o'er the garden-wall,
Bounding through the busy street,
    Ranging cellar, shed, and hall.

Never count the moments lost,
Never mind the time it costs:
Little feet will go astray —
Guide them, mother, while you may.

Mother, watch the little hand
　　Picking berries by the way,
Making houses in the sand,
　　Tossing up the fragrant hay.
Never dare the question ask,
" Why to me this weary task ? "
These same little hands may prove
Messengers of light and love.

Mother, watch the little heart
　　Beating soft and warm for you;
Wholesome lessons now impart:
　　Keep, oh, keep that young heart true,
Extricating every weed ;
Sowing good and precious seed,
Harvest rich you then may see,
Ripening for eternity.

NOT A CHILD.

ALGERNON CHARLES SWINBURNE.

" Not a child; I call myself a boy,"
Says my king, with accents stern yet mild,
Now nine years have brought him change of joy;
　　" Not a child."

How could reason be so far beguiled,
Err so far from senses' safe employ,
Stray so far from truth or run so wild?

Seeing his face bent over book or toy,
"Child" I called him smiling: but he smiled
Back, as one too high for vain annoy —
        "Not a child!"

CROWNS FOR CHILDREN.

ANONYMOUS.

THE children crowned themselves with roses,
    And all the roses died!
Pale on the soft brown locks they lay,
Like a dream of spring on a cold white day,
    In the barren winter-tide.
        Throw the fading vision by!
        Make a crown that cannot die.

The children crowned themselves with diamonds,
    And could not bear the weight;
Down they droop their weary curls,
Like a leaf that falls or a sail that furls,
    When the night is dark and late.
        Throw away the useless things!
        Crowns should be as light as wings.

The children crowned themselves with wishes,
    And every wish came true;

Love lies soft on each fair head,
Kisses dry the tears they shed, —
   Hope each day is new.
      Keep that crown, nor keep in vain!
      If it dies, it grows again.

WISHING.

WILLIAM ALLINGHAM.

RING-TING! I wish I were a Primrose,
A bright yellow Primrose, blowing in the spring!
   The stooping bough above me,
   The wandering bee to love me,
The fern and moss to creep across,
   And the Elm-tree for our king!

Nay, — stay! I wish I were an Elm-tree,
A great lofty Elm-tree, with green leaves gay!
   The winds would set them dancing,
   The sun and moonshine glance in,
And birds would house among the boughs,
   And sweetly sing.

Oh, no! I wish I were a Robin, —
A Robin, or a little Wren, everywhere to go,
   Through forest, field, or garden,
   And ask no leave or pardon,
Till winter comes with icy thumbs
   To ruffle up our wing!

Well, — tell! where should I fly to,
Where go sleep in the dark wood or dell?
　　Before the day was over,
　　Home must come the rover,
For mother's kiss, — sweeter this
　　Than any other thing.

TIRED OF PLAY.

N. P. WILLIS.

TIRED of play! tired of play!
What hast thou done this livelong day?
The bird is hushed, and so is the bee,
The sun is creeping up steeple and tree;
The doves have flown to the sheltering eaves,
And the nests are dark with the drooping leaves;
Twilight gathers, and day is done:
How hast thou spent it, precious one?

Playing?　But what hast thou done beside,
To tell thy mother at eventide?
What promise of morn is left unbroken?
What kind word to thy playmate spoken?
Whom hast thou pitied, and whom forgiven?
How with thy faults has duty striven?
What hast thou learned by field and hill,
By greenwood path and by singing rill?

There will come an end to a longer day,
That will find thee tired, but not of play.

Well for thee, then, if thy lips can tell
A tale like this of a day spent well.
If thine open hand hath relieved distress,
If thy pity hath sprung, at wretchedness,
If thou hast forgiven the sore offence,
And humbled thy heart with penitence;
If nature's voices have spoken to thee,
With their holy meanings, eloquently;
If every creature hath won thy love,
From the creeping worm to the brooding dove;
And never a sad, low-spoken word
Hath plead with thy human heart unheard;—
Then, when the night steals on as now,
It will bring relief to thine aching brow,
And with joy and peace at the thought of rest,
Thou wilt sink to sleep on thy mother's breast.

LITTLE MOMENTS.

ANONYMOUS.

LITTLE moments, how they fly,
Golden-wingèd, flitting by,
Bearing many things for me
Into vast eternity!

Never do they wait to ask
If completed is my task,
Whether gathering grain or weeds,
Doing good or evil deeds;
Onward haste they evermore,
Adding all unto their store!

And the little moments keep
Record, if we wake or sleep,
Of our every thought and deed,
For us all some time to read.

Artists are the moments too,
Ever painting something new,
On the walls and in the air,
Painting pictures everywhere!

If we smile or if we frown,
Little moments put it down,
And the angel, memory,
Guards the whole eternally!

Let us then so careful be,
That they bear for you and me,
On their little noiseless wings
Only good and pleasant things;
And that pictures which they paint
Have no background of complaint:
So the angel, memory,
May not blush for you and me!

GOOD–NIGHT AND GOOD–MORNING.

LORD HOUGHTON.

A FAIR little girl sat under a tree,
Sewing as long as her eyes could see;
Then smoothed her work and folded it right,
And said, "Dear work, good-night, good-night!"

Such a number of rooks came over her head,
Crying "Caw! Caw!" on their way to bed,
She said, as she watched their curious flight,
"Little black things, good-night, good-night!"

The horses neighed, and the oxen lowed,
The sheep's "Bleat! Bleat!" came over the road;
All seeming to say, with a quiet delight,
"Good little girl, good-night, good-night!"

She did not say to the sun, "Good-night!"
Though she saw him there like a ball of light;
For she knew he had God's time to keep
All over the world, and never could sleep.

The tall pink foxglove bowed his head;
The violets curtsied, and went to bed;
And good little Lucy tied up her hair,
And said, on her knees, her favorite prayer.

And, while on her pillow she softly lay,
She knew nothing more till again it was day;
And all things said to the beautiful sun,
"Good-morning, good-morning! our work is begun!"

CHOOSING A NAME.

MARY LAMB.

I HAVE got a new-born sister;
I was nigh the first that kissed her
When the nursing-woman brought her
To papa — his infant daughter!

And papa has made the offer,
I shall have the naming of her.

Now I wonder what would please her —
Charlotte, Julia, or Louisa?
Ann and Mary, they're too common;
Joan's too formal for a woman;
Jane's a prettier name beside;
But we had a Jane that died.
They would say, if 'twas Rebecca,
That she was a little Quaker.

Edith's pretty, but that looks
Better in old English books;
Ellen's left off long ago;
Blanche is out of fashion now.
None that I have named as yet
Are so good as Margaret.

Emily is neat and fine;
What do you think of Caroline?
How I'm puzzled and perplexed
What to choose or think of next!
I am in a little fever
Lest the name that I should give her
Should disgrace her or defame her —
I will leave papa to name her!

Be gentle! The sea is held in check, not by a wall
of brick, but by a beach of sand.

A NOVEMBER CHILD.

R. W. GILDER.

NOVEMBER winds, blow mild
On this new-born child!
Spirit of the autumn wood,
Make her gentle, make her good!
Still attend her,
And befriend her,
Fill her days with warmth and color;
Keep her safe from winter's dolor.
On thy bosom
Hide this blossom,
Safe from summer's rain and thunder!
When these eyes of light and wonder
Tire at last of earthly places —
Full of years and full of graces —
Then, O then
Take her back to heaven again!

BABY'S SHOES.

W. C. BENNETT.

OH, those little, those little blue shoes!
Those shoes that no little feet use;
    Oh, the price were high
    That those shoes could buy, —
Those little blue, unused shoes.

For they hold the small shape of feet
That no more their mother's eyes meet;
    That by God's good will
    Years since grew still,
And ceased from their totter so sweet.

And oh, since that baby slept
So hushed, how the mother has kept,
    With a tearful pleasure,
    That dear little treasure,
And over them thought and wept!

For they mind her for evermore
Of a patter along the floor;
    And blue eyes she sees
    Look up from her knees,
With the look that in life they wore.

As they lie before her there,
There babbles from chair to chair,
    A little sweet face
    That's a gleam in the place,
With its little gold curls of hair.

Then, oh, wonder not that her heart
From all else would rather part,
    Than those tiny blue shoes
    That no little feet use,
And whose sight makes such fond tears start.

PHILIP, MY KING.

DINAH MARIA MULOCK.

LOOK at me with thy large brown eyes,
  Philip, my King!
For round thee the purple shadow lies
Of babyhood's regal dignities.
Lay on my neck thy tiny hand,
 With Love's invisible sceptre laden;
I am thine Esther to command
 Till thou shalt find thy queen hand-maiden,
  Philip, my King!

Oh, the day when thou goest a-wooing,
  Philip, my King!
When those beautiful lips are suing,
And, some gentle heart's bars undoing,
Thou dost enter, love-crowned, and there
 Sittest all glorified! — Rule kindly,
Tenderly, over thy kingdom fair;
 For we that love, ah! we love so blindly,
  Philip, my King!

I gaze from thy sweet mouth up to thy brow,
  Philip, my King!
Ay, there lies the spirit, all sleeping now,
That may rise like a giant, and make men bow
As to one God-throned amidst his peers.
 My Saul, than thy brethren higher and fairer,
Let me behold thee in coming years!

Yet thy head needeth a circlet rarer,
     Philip, my King —

A wreath, not of gold, but palm! One day,
     Philip, my King!
Thou too must tread, as we tread, a way
Thorny, and bitter, and cold, and gray;
Rebels within thee, and foes without
     Will snatch at thy crown; but go on, glorious
Martyr, yet monarch! till angels shout,
     As thou sittest at the feet of God victorious,
     "Philip, the King!"

SUMMER CHANGES.

PHILIP BOURKE MARSTON.[1]

SANG the lily and sang the rose,
Out of the heart of my garden close:
     "O joy, O joy of the summer tide!"
Sang the wind, as it moved above them:
"Roses were sent for the sun to love them,
     Dear little buds, in the leaves that hide!"

Sang the trees, as they rustled together:
"O the joy of the summer weather!
     Roses and lilies, how do you fare?"

---

[1] It was to Philip Bourke Marston that Miss Mulock's poem, "Philip, my King," was addressed in his infancy. In after life he met with many misfortunes, and entirely lost his eye-sight. He was frequently called "the blind poet."

Sang the red rose, and sang the white:
"Glad we are of the sun's large light,
  And the songs of the birds that dart through the air."

Lily, and rose, and tall green tree,
Swaying boughs where the bright birds be,
  Thrilled by music and thrilled by wings,
How glad they were on that summer day!
Little they recked of cold skies and gray,
  Or the dreary dirge that a storm-wind sings!

Golden butterflies gleam in the sun,
Laugh at the flowers, and kiss each one;
  And great bees come, with their sleepy tune,
To sip their honey and circle round;
And the flowers are lulled by that drowsy sound,
  And fall asleep in the heart of the noon.

A small white cloud in a sky of blue:
Roses and lilies, what will they do?
  For a wind springs up and sings in the trees.
Down comes the rain; the garden's awake:
Roses and lilies begin to quake,
  That were rocked to sleep by the gentle breeze.

Ah, roses and lilies! Each delicate petal
The wind and the rain with fear unsettle —
  This way and that way the tall trees sway:
But the wind goes by, and the rain stops soon,
And smiles again the face of the noon,
  And the flowers grow glad in the sun's warm ray.

Sing, my lilies, and sing, my roses,
With never a dream that the summer closes!
   But the trees are old; and I fancy they tell,
Each unto each, how the summer flies:
They remember the last year's wintry skies;
   But that summer returns the trees know well.

THE BLIND BOY.

COLLEY CIBBER.

O, SAY, what is that thing called light,
   Which I must ne'er enjoy?
What are the blessings of the sight?
   O tell your poor blind boy!

You talk of wondrous things you see;
   You say the sun shines bright;
I feel him warm, but how can he
   Make either day or night?

My day and night myself I make,
   Whene'er I sleep or play,
And could I always keep awake,
   With me 'twere always day.

With heavy sighs I often hear
   You mourn my hapless woe;
But sure with patience I can bear
   A loss I ne'er can know.

Then let not what I cannot have
  My peace of mind destroy;
While thus I sing, I am a king,
  Although a poor blind boy!

I REMEMBER, I REMEMBER.

THOMAS HOOD.

I REMEMBER, I remember
  The house where I was born;
The little window where the sun
  Came peeping in at morn;
He never came a wink too soon,
  Nor brought too long a day;
But now, I often wish the night
  Had borne my breath away!

I remember, I remember
  The roses, red and white,
The violets, and the lily-cups —
  Those flowers made of light!
The lilacs where the robin built,
  And where my brother set
The laburnum, on his birthday, —
  The tree is living yet!

I remember, I remember
  Where I was used to swing,
And thought the air must rush as fresh
  To swallows on the wing;

My spirit flew in feathers then,
   That is so heavy now,
And summer pools could hardly cool
   The fever of my brow!

I remember, I remember
   The fir-trees dark and high;
I used to think their slender tops
   Were close against the sky.
It was a childish ignorance,
   But now 'tis little joy
To know I'm farther off from heaven
   Than when I was a boy.

THE OLD OAKEN BUCKET.

Samuel Woodworth.

How dear to my heart are the scenes of my childhood,
   When fond recollection presents them to view!
The orchard, the meadow, the deep-tangled wild-wood,
   And every loved spot which my infancy knew;
The wide-spreading pond, and the mill that stood by it;
   The bridge, and the rock where the cataract fell;
The cot of my father, the dairy-house nigh it,
   And e'en the rude bucket which hung in the well;
The old oaken bucket, the iron-bound bucket,
   The moss-covered bucket which hung in the well.

That moss-covered vessel I hail as a treasure;
   For often at noon when returned from the field,

I found it the source of an exquisite pleasure,
   The purest and sweetest that nature can yield.
How ardent I seized it, with hands that were glowing,
   And quick to the white-pebbled bottom it fell;
Then soon with the emblem of truth overflowing,
   And dripping with coolness, it rose from the well.
The old oaken bucket, the iron-bound bucket,
   The moss-covered bucket arose from the well.

How sweet from the green mossy brim to receive it,
   As poised on the curb, it inclined to my lips!
Not a full-blushing goblet could tempt me to leave it,
   Though filled with the nectar that Jupiter sips.
And now, far removed from that loved situation,
   The tear of regret will intrusively swell,
As fancy reverts to my father's plantation,
   And sighs for the bucket that hangs in the well;
The old oaken bucket, the iron-bound bucket,
   The moss-covered bucket that hangs in the well.

HOME, SWEET HOME.

JOHN HOWARD PAYNE.

'MID pleasures and palaces though we may roam,
Be it ever so humble, there's no place like home!
A charm from the skies seems to hallow us there,
Which, seek through the world, is ne'er met with else-
     where.
      Home, home, sweet home!
      There's no place like home!

An exile from home, splendor dazzles in vain:
Ah, give me my lowly thatched cottage again!
The birds singing sweetly that come at my call —
Give me them, and that peace of mind, dearer than all.
      Home, home, sweet home!
      There's no place like home!

FAREWELL ADVICE.

CHARLES KINGSLEY.

FAREWELL, dear child, I have no song to give thee.
  No lark could pipe to skies so dull and gray:
But ere we part one lesson I would leave thee,
      For every day.

Be good, sweet maid, and let who will be clever.
  Do noble things, not dream them all day long:
And so make life, death, and that vast forever,
      One grand, sweet song.

LIFE'S "GOOD–MORNING."

A. L. BARBAULD.

LIFE! we have been long together,
Through pleasant and through cloudy weather.
'Tis hard to part when friends are dear;
Perhaps 'twill cost a sigh, a tear;
Then steal away, give little warning,
Choose thine own time;
Say not " Good-night," but in some brighter clime
Bid me " Good-morning."

NATURE.

PLAYTIME AND MEMORY RHYMES.

SCULPTURE BY LUCA DELLA ROBBIA. FLORENCE.

NATURE.

——∘∘⦂❀⦂∘∘——

THE GREENWOOD TREE.

UNDER the greenwood tree
Who loves to lie with me,
And tune his merry note
Unto the sweet bird's throat,
Come hither, come hither, come hither;
    Here shall he see
    No enemy,
But winter and rough weather.

Who doth ambition shun,
And loves to lie in the sun,
Seeking the food he eats,
And pleased with what he gets,
Come hither, come hither, come hither!
    Here shall he see
    No enemy,
But winter and rough weather.

HARK!

WILLIAM SHAKESPEARE.

HARK, Hark! the lark at heaven's gate sings,
  And Phœbus 'gins arise,
His steeds to water at those springs
  On chaliced flowers that lies:
And winking Mary-buds begin
  To ope their golden eyes;
With everything that pretty bin,
  My lady sweet, arise:
    Arise, arise!

HIE AWAY.

SIR WALTER SCOTT.

HIE away, hie away!
Over bank and over brae,
Where the copsewood is the greenest,
Where the fountains glisten sheenest,
Where the lady fern grows strongest,
Where the morning dew lies longest,
Where the blackcock sweetest sips it,
Where the fairy latest trips it:
Hie to haunts right seldom seen,
Lovely, lonesome, cool, and green,
Over bank and over brae,
Hie away, hie away!

MY HEART'S IN THE HIGHLANDS.

ROBERT BURNS.

MY heart's in the Highlands, my heart is not here;
My heart's in the Highlands a-chasing the deer;
Chasing the wild deer, and following the roe,
My heart's in the Highlands wherever I go.
Farewell to the Highlands, farewell to the North,
The birthplace of valor, the country of worth;
Wherever I wander, wherever I rove,
The hills of the Highlands forever I love.

Farewell to the mountains high covered with snow;
Farewell to the straths and green valleys below;
Farewell to the forests and wild-hanging woods;
Farewell to the torrents and loud-pouring floods.
My heart's in the Highlands, my heart is not here,
My heart's in the Highlands a-chasing the deer;
Chasing the wild deer and following the roe,
My heart's in the Highlands wherever I go.

A VISIT FROM THE SEA.

ROBERT LOUIS STEVENSON.

FAR from the loud sea-beaches,
    Where he goes fishing and crying,
Here in the inland garden,
    Why is the sea-gull flying?

Here are no fish to dive for:
　Here is the corn and lea;
Here are the green trees rustling.
　Hie away home to sea!

Fresh is the river water,
　And quiet among the rushes;
This is no home for the sea-gull,
　But for the rooks and thrushes.

Pity the bird that has wandered!
　Pity the sailor ashore!
Hurry him home to the ocean,
　Let him come here no more!

High on the sea-cliff ledges
　The white gulls are trooping and crying;
Here among rooks and roses,
　Why is the sea-gull flying?

THE BROOK.

ALFRED TENNYSON.

I COME from haunts of coot and hern;
　I make a sudden sally,
And sparkle out among the fern
　To bicker down a valley.

By thirty hills I hurry down,
　Or slip between the ridges;

By twenty thorps, a little town,
   And half a hundred bridges.

Till last by Philip's farm I flow
   To join the brimming river;
For men may come, and men may go,
   But I go on forever.

I chatter over stony ways,
   In little sharps and trebles;
I bubble into eddying bays;
   I babble on the pebbles.

With many a curve my bank I fret
   By many a field and fallow,
And many a fairy foreland set
   With willow-weed and mallow.

I chatter, chatter, as I flow
   To join the brimming river;
For men may come, and men may go,
   But I go on forever.

I wind about, and in and out,
   With here a blossom sailing,
And here and there a lusty trout,
   And here and there a grayling,

And here and there a foamy flake
   Upon me as I travel,
With many a silvery waterbreak
   Above the golden gravel,

And draw them all along, and flow
  To join the brimming river;
For men may come, and men may go,
  But I go on forever.

I steal by lawns and grassy plots,
  I slide by hazel covers,
I move the sweet forget-me-nots
  That grow for happy lovers.

I slip, I slide, I gloom, I glance,
  Among my skimming swallows;
I make the netted sunbeam dance
  Against my sandy shallows.

I murmur under moon and stars
  In brambly wildernesses;
I linger by my shingly bars;
  I loiter round my cresses;

And out again I curve and flow
  To join the brimming river;
For men may come, and men may go,
  But I go on forever.

STARS.

BARRY CORNWALL.

THEY glide upon their endless way,
  Forever calm, forever bright;
No blind hurry, no delay,

Mark the Daughters of the Night;
They follow in the track of Day,
    In divine delight.

Shine on, sweet-orbèd Souls for aye,
    Forever calm, forever bright;
We ask not whither lies your way,
    Nor whence ye came, nor what your light.
Be — still a dream throughout the day,
    A blessing through the night.

THE FOUNTAIN.

JAMES RUSSELL LOWELL.

INTO the sunshine,
    Full of the light,
Leaping and flashing
    From morn till night!

Into the moonlight,
    Whiter than snow,
Waving so flower-like
    When the winds blow!

Into the starlight,
    Rushing in spray,
Happy at midnight,
    Happy by day!

Ever in motion,
    Blithesome and cheery,

Still climbing heavenward,
　Never aweary;

Glad of all weathers,
　Still seeming best,
Upward or downward
　Motion thy rest;

Full of a nature
　Nothing can tame,
Changed every moment,
　Ever the same;

Ceaseless aspiring,
　Ceaseless content,
Darkness or sunshine
　Thy element;

Glorious fountain!
　Let my heart be
Fresh, changeful, constant,
　Upward like thee!

MARCH.

WILLIAM WORDSWORTH.

THE cock is crowing,
The stream is flowing,
The small birds twitter,
The lake doth glitter,

The green field sleeps in the sun;
   The oldest and youngest
     Are at work with the strongest;
     The cattle are grazing,
     Their heads never raising;
There are forty feeding like one.

     Like an army defeated
     The snow hath retreated,
     And now doth fare ill
     On the top of the bare hill;
The ploughboy is whooping — anon — anon!
     There's joy on the mountains;
     There's life in the fountains;
     Small clouds are sailing,
     Blue sky prevailing;
The rain is over and gone.

THE SHELL.

ALFRED TENNYSON.

SEE what a lovely shell,
Small and pure as a pearl,
Lying close to my foot,
Frail, but a work divine,
Made so fairily well
With delicate spire and whorl,
How exquisitely minute,
A miracle of design!

What is it? a learned man
Could give it a clumsy name.
Let him name it who can,
The beauty would be the same.

The tiny cell is forlorn,
Void of the little living will
That made it stir on the shore.
Did he stand at the diamond door
Of his house in a rainbow frill?
Did he push, when he was uncurled,
A golden foot or a fairy horn
Through his dim water-world?

Slight, to be crush'd with a tap
Of my finger-nail on the sand!
Small, but a work divine!
Frail, but of force to withstand,
Year upon year, the shock
Of cataract seas that snap
The three-decker's oaken spine
Athwart the ledges of rock,
Here on the Breton strand!

THE BROOM FLOWER.

MARY HOWITT.

O THE Broom, the yellow Broom,
    The ancient poet sung it,
And dear it is on summer days
    To lie at rest among it.

I know the realms where people say
  The flowers have not their fellow;
I know where they shine out like suns,
  The purple and the yellow.

I know where ladies live enchained
  In luxury's silken fetters,
And flowers as bright as glittering gems
  Are used for written letters.

But ne'er was flower so fair as this,
  In modern days or olden;
It groweth on its nodding stem
  Like to a garland golden.

And all about my mother's door
  Shine out its glittering bushes,
And down the glen, where clear as light
  The mountain water gushes.

Take all the rest, but give me this,
  And the bird that nestles in it.
I love it for it loves the Broom,
  The green and yellow linnet.

Well, call the rose the queen of flowers,
  And boast of that of Sharon,
Of lilies like to marble cups
  And the golden rod of Aaron.

I care not how these flowers may be
  Beloved of man and woman;

The Broom it is the flower for me,
That groweth on the common.

O the Broom, the yellow Broom,
The ancient poet sung it,
And dear it is on summer days
To lie at rest among it.

SEPTEMBER.

H. H.

THE golden-rod is yellow,
The corn is turning brown,
The trees in apple orchards
With fruit are bending down.

The gentian's bluest fringes
Are curling in the sun,
In dusky pods the milkweed
Its hidden silk has spun.

The sedges flaunt their harvest
In every meadow-nook,
And asters by the brookside
Make asters in the brook.

By all these lovely tokens
September days are here,
With summer's best of wealth
And autumn's best of cheer.

LADY MOON.

LORD HOUGHTON.

I SEE the Moon, and the Moon sees me;
God bless the Moon, and God bless me!

— OLD RHYME.

LADY MOON, Lady Moon, where are you roving?
"Over the sea."
Lady Moon, Lady Moon, whom are you loving?
"All that love me."

Are you not tired with rolling, and never
Resting to sleep?
Why look so pale and so sad, as forever
Wishing to weep?

"Ask me not this, little child, if you love me:
You are too bold:
I must obey my dear Father above me,
And do as I'm told."

Lady Moon, Lady Moon, where are you roving?
"Over the sea."
Lady Moon, Lady Moon, whom are you loving?
"All that love me."

ANSWER TO A CHILD'S QUESTION.

SAMUEL TAYLOR COLERIDGE.

Do you ask what the birds say? The sparrow, the dove,
The linnet, and thrush say, "I love and I love!"
In the winter they're silent, the wind is so strong;
What it says I don't know, but it sings a loud song.
But green leaves and blossoms, and sunny warm
       weather,
And singing and loving, all come back together;
Then the lark is so brimful of gladness and love,
The green fields below him, the blue sky above,
That he sings, and he sings, and forever sings he,
"I love my Love, and my Love loves me."

THE BALLAD OF THE THRUSH.

AUSTIN DOBSON.

ACROSS the noisy street,
I hear him careless throw
One warning utterance sweet;
Then, faint at first and low,
The full notes closer grow —
Hark! what a torrent gush!
They pour, they overflow —
Sing on, — sing on, O Thrush!

What trick, what dream's deceit
Has fooled his fancy so
To scorn of dust and heat?

I, prisoned here below,
Feel the fresh breezes blow;
And see, thro' flag and rush,
Cool water sliding slow —
Sing on, — sing on, O Thrush!

Sing on, what though thou beat
On that dull bar, thy foe!
Somewhere the green boughs meet
Beyond the roofs a-row;
Somewhere the blue skies show;
Somewhere no black walls crush
Poor hearts with helpless woe —
Sing on, — sing on, O Thrush!

Bird, though they come, we know,
The empty cage, the hush;
Still, ere the brief day go,
Sing on, — sing on, O Thrush!

LADY–BIRD, LADY–BIRD.

CAROLINE B. SOUTHEY.

LADY-BIRD, lady-bird! fly away home!
The field-mouse has gone to her nest,
The daisies have shut up their sleepy red eyes,
And the bees and the birds are at rest.

Lady-bird, lady-bird! fly away home!
The glow-worm is lighting her lamp,

The dew's falling fast, and your fine speckled wings
　　Will flag with the close clinging damp.

Lady-bird, lady-bird! fly away home!
　　Good luck if you reach it at last!
The owl's come abroad, and the bat's on the roam,
　　Sharp set from their Ramazan fast.

Lady-bird, lady-bird! fly away home!
　　The fairy bells tinkle afar!
Make haste, or they'll catch you, and harness you
　　　fast
　　With a cobweb to Oberon's car.

Lady-bird, lady-bird! fly away home!
　　To your house in the old willow tree,
Where your children so dear have invited the ant
　　And a few cosey neighbors to tea.

Lady-bird, lady-bird! fly away home!
　　And if not gobbled up by the way,
Nor yoked by the fairies to Oberon's car,
　　You're in luck!—and that's all I've to say!

AN EPITAPH ON A ROBIN REDBREAST.

Samuel Rogers.

Tread lightly here; for here, 'tis said,
When piping winds are hush'd around,
A small note wakes from underground,
Where now his tiny bones are laid.

No more in lone or leafless groves,
With ruffled wing and faded breast,
His friendless, homeless spirit roves;
Gone to the world where birds are blest!

Where never cat glides o'er the green,
Or school-boy's giant form is seen;
But love, and joy, and smiling Spring
Inspire their little souls to sing!

THE CUCKOO.

OLD ENGLISH.

In April
Come he will,
In flow'ry May
He sings all day,
In leafy June
He changes his tune,
In bright July
He's ready to fly,
In August
Go he must.

THE LITTLE BIRD.

MARTIN LUTHER.

ONE evening when Luther saw a little bird perched
on a tree to roost there for the night, he said: " This

little bird has had its supper and now it is getting ready to go to sleep here, quite secure and content, never troubling itself what its food will be, or where its lodging on the morrow. Like David it 'abides under the shadow of the Almighty.' It sits on its little twig content, and lets God take care!"

THE EAGLE.

ALFRED TENNYSON.

He clasps the crag with hookèd hands;
Close to the sun in lonely lands,
Ring'd with the azure world, he stands.

The wrinkled sea beneath him crawls;
He watches from his mountain walls;
And like a thunderbolt he falls.

THE DOVE.

JOHN KEATS.

I had a dove, and the sweet dove died;
   And I have thought it died of grieving:
O, what could it grieve for? Its feet were tied
   With a silken thread of my own hands' weaving;
Sweet little red feet! why should you die —
Why would you leave me, sweet bird! why?
You lived alone in the forest tree,

Why, pretty thing! would you not live with me?
I kiss'd you oft and gave you white peas;
Why not live sweetly, as in the green trees?

THE SANDPIPER.

CELIA THAXTER.

ACROSS the lonely beach we flit,
   One little sandpiper and I,
And fast I gather, bit by bit,
   The scattered drift-wood, bleached and dry.
The wild waves reach their hands for it,
   The wild wind raves, the tide runs high,
As up and down the beach we flit,
   One little sandpiper and I.

Above our heads the sullen clouds
   Scud, black and swift, across the sky;
Like silent ghosts in misty shrouds
   Stand out the white light-houses high.
Almost as far as eye can reach
   I see the close-reefed vessels fly,
As fast we flit along the beach,
   One little sandpiper and I.

I watch him as he skims along,
   Uttering his sweet and mournful cry;
He starts not at my fitful song,
   Nor flash of fluttering drapery.

He has no thought of any wrong,
　　He scans me with a fearless eye;
Stanch friends are we, well tried and strong,
　　The little sandpiper and I.

Comrade, where wilt thou be to-night,
　　When the loosed storm breaks furiously?
My drift-wood fire will burn so bright!
　　To what warm shelter canst thou fly?
I do not fear for thee, though wroth
　　The tempest rushes through the sky;
For are we not God's children both,
　　Thou, little sandpiper, and I?

THE SKYLARK.

JAMES HOGG.

BIRD of the wilderness,
　　Blithesome and cumberless,
Sweet be thy matin o'er moorland and lea!
　　Emblem of happiness,
　　Blest is thy dwelling-place,—
O to abide in the desert with thee!
　　Wild is thy lay and loud
　　Far in the downy cloud,
Love gives it energy, love gave it birth.
　　Where, on thy dewy wing,
　　Where art thou journeying?
Thy lay is in heaven, thy love is on earth.

O'er fell and fountain sheen,
O'er moor and mountain green,
O'er the red streamer that heralds the day,
Over the cloudlet dim,
Over the rainbow's rim,
Musical cherub, soar, singing, away!
Then, when the gloaming comes,
Low in the heather blooms,
Sweet will thy welcome and bed of love be!
Emblem of happiness,
Blest is thy dwelling-place,
O to abide in the desert with thee!

ROBIN REDBREAST.

William Allingham.

Goodby, goodby to Summer!
For Summer's nearly done;
The garden smiling faintly,
Cool breezes in the sun;
Our thrushes now are silent,
Our swallows flown away, —
But Robin's here in coat of brown,
And scarlet breast-knot gay.
Robin, Robin Redbreast,
O Robin dear!
Robin sings so sweetly
In the falling of the year.
Bright yellow, red, and orange,

The leaves come down in hosts;
The trees are Indian princes,
　　But soon they'll turn to ghosts;
The leathery pears and apples
　　Hang russet on the bough;
It's Autumn, Autumn, Autumn late,
　　'Twill soon be Winter now.
Robin, Robin Redbreast,
　　O Robin dear!
And what will this poor Robin do?
　　For pinching days are near.

The fire-side for the cricket,
　　The wheat-stack for the mouse,
When trembling night-winds whistle
　　And moan all round the house.
The frosty ways like iron,
　　The branches plumed with snow, —
Alas! in winter dead and dark,
　　Where can poor Robin go?　.
Robin, Robin Redbreast,
　　O Robin dear!
And a crumb of bread for Robin,
　　His little heart to cheer.

WHEN daffodils begin to peer, with heigh! the doxy
　　over the dale,
Why then comes in the sweet o' the year, for the
　　red blood reigns in the winter's pale.

—WILLIAM SHAKESPEARE.

THE BIRD.

WILLIAM ALLINGHAM.

" BIRDIE, Birdie, will you, pet ?
Summer is far and far away yet.
You'll have silken quilts and a velvet bed,
And a pillow of satin for your head."

" I'd rather sleep in the ivy wall :
No rain comes through, though I hear it fall ;
The sun peeps gay at dawn of day,
And I sing, and wing away, away ! "

" O Birdie, Birdie, will you, pet ?
Diamond stones and amber and jet
We'll string on a necklace fair and fine,
To please this pretty bird of mine."

" Oh ! thanks for diamonds, and thanks for jet ;
But here is something daintier yet, —
A feather necklace, round and round,
That I would not sell for a thousand pound ! "

" O Birdie, Birdie, won't you, pet ?
We'll buy you a dish of silver fret,
A golden cup and an ivory seat,
And carpets soft beneath your feet."

" Can running water be drunk from gold ?
Can a silver dish the forest hold ?
A rocking twig is the finest chair,
And the softest paths lie through the air :
Goodby, goodby, to my lady fair."

THE OWL.

ALFRED TENNYSON.

WHEN cats run home and light is come,
And dew is cold upon the ground,
And the far-off stream is dumb,
  And the whirring sail goes round;
  And the whirring sail goes round;
    Alone and warming his five wits,
    The white owl in the belfry sits.

When merry milkmaids click the latch,
  And rarely smells the new-mown hay,
And the cock hath sung beneath the thatch
  Twice or thrice his roundelay,
  Twice or thrice his roundelay;
    Alone and warming his five wits,
    The white owl in the belfry sits.

FLOWER IN THE CRANNIED WALL.

ALFRED TENNYSON.

FLOWER in the crannied wall,
I pluck you out of the crannies;—
Hold you here, root and all, in my hand,
Little flower—but if I could understand
What you are, root and all, and all in all,
I should know what God and man is.

THE SUCCORY.

MARGARET DELAND.

Oh not in ladies' gardens,
My peasant posy,
Smile thy dear blue eyes;
Nor only — nearer to the skies —
In upland pastures,
Dim and sweet;
But by the dusty road,
Where tired feet
Toil to and fro,
Where flaunting sin
May see thy heavenly hue,
Or weary sorrow look from thee
Toward that tenderer blue.

LITTLE WHITE LILY.

GEORGE MACDONALD.

Little white Lily
Sat by a stone,
Drooping and waiting
Till the sun shone.
Little white Lily
Sunshine has fed;
Little white Lily
Is lifting her head.

Little white Lily
Said, "It is good —
Little white Lily's
Clothing and food."
Little white Lily
Drest like a bride!
Shining with whiteness,
And crowned beside!

Little white Lily
Droopeth with pain,
Waiting and waiting
For the wet rain.
Little white Lily
Holdeth her cup;
Rain is fast falling
And filling it up.

Little white Lily
Said, "Good again —
When I am thirsty
To have fresh rain!
Now I am stronger;
Now I am cool;
Heat cannot burn me,
My veins are so full."

Little white Lily
Smells very sweet:
On her head sunshine,
Rain at her feet.

"Thanks to the sunshine,
Thanks to the rain!
Little white Lily
Is happy again!"

TO VIOLETS.

ROBERT HERRICK.

WELCOME, Maids of Honor,
You do bring
In the spring
And wait upon her.

She has virgins many,
Fresh and fair;
Yet you are
More sweet than any.

Y' are the Maiden Posies
And so graced
To be placed
'Fore damask roses.

Yet, though thus respected,
By and by
Ye do lie,
Poor girls, neglected.

VIOLETS.

J. Moultrie.

Under the green hedges after the snow,
There do the dear little violets grow,
Hiding their modest and beautiful heads
Under the hawthorn in soft mossy beds.

Sweet as the roses, and blue as the sky,
Down there do the dear little violets lie;
Hiding their heads where they scarce may be seen,
By the leaves you may know where the violet hath been.

THE RIVER.

Caroline B. Southey.

River! River! little River!
  Bright you sparkle on your way,
O'er the yellow pebbles dancing,
Through the flowers and foliage glancing,
    Like a child at play.

River! River! swelling River!
  On you rush o'er rough and smooth —
Louder, faster, brawling, leaping
Over rocks, by rose-banks sweeping,
    Like impetuous youth.

River! River! brimming River!
  Broad and deep and *still* as Time;
Seeming *still* — yet still in motion,

Tending onward to the ocean,
  Just like mortal prime.

River! River! rapid River!
  Swifter now you slip away;
Swift and silent as an arrow,
Through a channel dark and narrow,
    Like life's closing day.

River! River! headlong River!
  Down you dash into the sea;
Sea, that line hath never sounded,
Sea, that voyage hath never rounded,
    Like eternity.

THE SPACIOUS FIRMAMENT ON HIGH.

JOSEPH ADDISON.

THE spacious firmament on high,
With all the blue ethereal sky,
And spangled heavens, a shining frame,
Their great Original proclaim.
The unwearied sun from day to day
Does his Creator's power display,
And publishes to every land
The work of an Almighty hand.

Soon as the evening shades prevail,
The moon takes up the wondrous tale,
And nightly to the listening earth
Repeats the story of her birth;

Whilst all the stars that round her burn,
And all the planets in their turn,
Confirm the tidings as they roll,
And spread the truth from pole to pole.

What though in solemn silence, all
Move round this dark, terrestrial ball?
What though no real voice nor sound
Amidst their radiant orbs be found?
In Reason's ear they all rejoice,
And utter forth a glorious voice,
Forever singing as they shine:
"The hand that made us is divine!"

THE RAINBOW.

John Keble.

A FRAGMENT of a rainbow bright
    Through the moist air I see,
All dark and damp on yonder height,
    All bright and clear to me.

An hour ago the storm was here,
    The gleam was far behind,
So will our joys and grief appear,
    When earth has ceased to blind.

Grief will be joy if on its edge
    Fall soft that holiest ray,
Joy will be grief if no faint pledge
    Be there of heavenly day.

THE HOUSEKEEPER.

Charles Lamb.

The frugal snail, with forecast of repose,
Carries his house with him where'er he goes;
Peeps out, — and if there comes a shower of rain,
Retreats to his small domicile again.
Touch but a tip of him, a horn — 'tis well, —
He curls up in his sanctuary shell.
He's his own landlord, his own tenant; stay
Long as he will, he dreads no Quarter Day.
Himself he boards and lodges; both invites
And feasts himself; sleeps with himself o' nights.
He spares the upholsterer trouble to procure
Chattels; himself is his own furniture,
And his sole riches. Wheresoe'er he roam, —
Knock when you will, — he's sure to be at home.

THE LION AND THE CUB.

John Gay.

A lion cub, of sordid mind,
Avoided all the lion kind;
Fond of applause, he sought the beasts
Of vulgar and ignoble feasts;
With asses all his time he spent,
Their club's perpetual president.
He caught their manners, looks, and airs;
An ass in everything but ears!

If e'er his Highness meant a joke,
They grinn'd applause before he spoke;
But at each word what shouts of praise;
"Goodness! how natural he brays!"
    Elate with flattery and conceit,
He seeks his royal sire's retreat;
Forward and fond to show his parts,
His Highness brays; the lion starts.
    "Puppy! that curs'd vociferation
Betrays thy life and conversation:
Coxcombs, an ever-noisy race,
Are trumpets of their own disgrace."
    "Why so severe?" the cub replies;
"Our senate always held me wise!"
    "How weak is pride," returns the sire:
"All fools are vain when fools admire!
But know, what stupid asses prize,
Lions and noble beasts despise."

THE TIGER.

WILLIAM BLAKE.

TIGER, tiger, burning bright
In the forest of the night!
What immortal hand or eye
Could frame thy fearful symmetry?

In what distant deeps or skies
Burnt the ardor of thine eyes?

On what wings dare he aspire —
What the hand dare seize the fire?

And what shoulder, and what art
Could twist the sinews of thy heart?
And when thy heart began to beat,
What dread hand form'd thy dread feet?

What the hammer, what the chain,
In what furnace was thy brain?
Did God smile his work to see?
Did He who made the lamb make thee?

THE KITTEN AND FALLING LEAVES.

WILLIAM WORDSWORTH.

SEE the kitten on the wall,
Sporting with the leaves that fall,
Withered leaves — one — two — and three —
From the lofty elder tree!
Through the calm and frosty air
Of this morning bright and fair,
Eddying round and round they sink
Softly, slowly: one might think
From the motions that are made,
Every little leaf conveyed
Sylph or fairy hither tending,
To this lower world descending,
Each invisible and mute,
In his wavering parachute.

But the kitten, how she starts,
Crouches, stretches, paws, and darts'
First at one, and then its fellow,
Just as light and just as yellow;
There are many now — now one —
Now they stop and there are none:
What intenseness of desire
In her upward eye of fire!
With a tiger-leap, half-way
Now she meets the coming prey,
Lets it go as fast, and then
Has it in her power again:
Now she works with three or four,
Like an Indian conjuror;
Quick as he in feats of art,
Far beyond in joy of heart.

APRIL IN ENGLAND.

ROBERT BROWNING.   EXTRACT.

OH, to be in England
   Now that April's there,
And whoever wakes in England
   Sees, some morning, unaware,
That the lowest boughs and the brushwood sheaf
Round the elm-tree bole are in tiny leaf,
While the chaffinch sings on the orchard bough
In England — now!

SPRING AND SUMMER.

Anonymous.

Spring is growing up,
  Isn't it a pity?
She was such a little thing,
  And so very pretty!
Summer is extremely grand,
  We must pay her duty;
(But it is to little Spring
  That she owes her beauty!)

All the buds are blown,
  Trees are dark and shady,
(It was Spring who dress'd them, though,
  Such a little lady!)
And the birds sing loud and sweet
  Their enchanting hist'ries.
(It was Spring who taught them, though,
  Such a singing mistress!)

From the glowing sky
  Summer shines above us;
Spring was such a little dear,
  But will Summer love us?
She is very beautiful,
  With her grown-up blisses,
Summer we must bow before;
  Spring we coaxed with kisses!

Spring is growing up,
   Leaving us so lonely,
In the place of little Spring
   We have Summer only!
Summer, with her lofty airs,
   And her stately paces,
In the place of little Spring,
   With her childish graces!

A MIDSUMMER SONG.

R. W. GILDER.

OH, father's gone to market-town: he was up before
   the day,
And Jamie's after robins, and the man is making hay,
And whistling down the hollow goes the boy that
   minds the mill,
While mother from the kitchen-door is calling with a
   will,
   "Polly!—Polly!—The cows are in the corn!
      Oh, where's Polly?"

From all the misty morning air there comes a summer
   sound,
A murmur as of waters, from skies and trees and ground.
The birds they sing upon the wing, the pigeons bill and
   coo;
And over hill and hollow rings again the loud halloo:
   "Polly!—Polly!—The cows are in the corn!
      Oh, where's Polly?"

Above the trees, the honey-bees swarm by with buzz
    and boom,
And in the field and garden a thousand blossoms bloom.
Within the farmer's meadow a brown-eyed daisy blows,
And down at the edge of the hollow a red and thorny
    rose.
    But Polly! — Polly! — The cows are in the corn!
      Oh, where's Polly?

How strange at such a time of day the mill should stop
    its clatter!
The farmer's wife is listening now, and wonders what's
    the matter.
Oh, wild the birds are singing in the wood and on the
    hill,
While whistling up the hollow goes the boy that minds
    the mill.
    But Polly! — Polly! — The cows are in the corn!
      Oh, where's Polly!

THE WAY FOR BILLY AND ME.

JAMES HOGG.

WHERE the pools are bright and deep,
Where the gray trout lies asleep,
Up the river and o'er the lea,
That's the way for Billy and me.

Where the blackbird sings the latest,
Where the hawthorn blooms the sweetest,

Where the nestlings chirp and flee,
That's the way for Billy and me.

Where the mowers mow the cleanest,
Where the hay lies thick and greenest;
There to trace the homeward bee,
That's the way for Billy and me.

Where the hazel bank is steepest,
Where the shadow lies the deepest,
Where the clustering nuts fall free,
That's the way for Billy and me.

Why the boys should drive away
Little maidens from their play,
Or love to banter and fight so well,
That's the thing I never could tell.

But this I know, I love to play,
Through the meadow, along the hay;
Up the water and o'er the lea,
That's the way for Billy and me.

A CHILD TO A ROSE.

ANONYMOUS.

WHITE Rose, talk to me!
　I don't know what to do.
Why do you say no word to me,
　Who say so much to you?
I'm bringing you a little rain,

And I shall be so proud
If, when you feel it on your face,
  You take me for a cloud.
Here I come so softly,
  You cannot hear me walking;
If I take you by surprise,
  I may catch you talking.

Tell all your thoughts to me,
  Whisper in my ear;
Talk against the winter,
  He shall never hear.
I can keep a secret
  Since I was five years old.
Tell if you were frighten'd
  When first you felt the cold;
And, in the splendid summer,
  While you flush and grow,
Are you ever out of heart
  Thinking of the snow?

Did it feel like dying
  When first your blossoms fell?
Did you know about the spring?
  Did the daisies tell?
If you had no notion,
  Only fear and doubt,
How I should have liked to see
  When you found it out!
Such a beautiful surprise!
  What must you have felt,

When your heart began to stir,
　　As the snow began to melt!

Do you mind the darkness
　　As I used to do?
You are not as old as I:
　　I can comfort you.
The little noises that you hear
　　Are winds that come and go.
The world is always kind and safe,
　　Whether you see or no;
And if you think that there are eyes
　　About you near and far,
Perhaps the fairies are watching,—
　　I know the angels are.

I think you must be lonely
　　When all the colors fail,
And moonlight makes the garden
　　So massy and so pale;
And *any*thing might come at last
　　Out of those heaps of shade.
I would stay beside you
　　If I were not afraid!
Children have no right to go
　　Abroad in night and gloom;
But you are as safe in the garden
　　As I am in my room.

White Rose, do you love me?
　　I only wish you'd say!
I would work hard to please you

If I but knew the way.
It seems so hard to be loving,
  And not a sign to see
But the silence and the sweetness
  For all as well as me.
I think you nearly perfect,
  In spite of all your scorns;
But, White Rose, if I were you,
  I *wouldn't* have those thorns!

STARS.

Anonymous.

How pretty is each little star,
  Each tiny twinkler, soft and meek!
Yet many in this world there are
  Who do not know that stars can speak.

To them the skies are meaningless,
  A star is not a living thing;
They cannot hear the messages
  Those shining creatures love to bring.

Hush! listen! ah! it will not do;
  You do but listen with your ears;
And stars are understood by few,
  For it must be the heart that hears.

Look up, not *only* with your eyes;
  Ah! do you hear a tender sound?
To hearts familiar with the skies,
  The stars are nearer than the ground.

THE WORLD.

" LILLIPUT LEVEE."

GREAT, wide, beautiful, wonderful World,
With the wonderful water round you curled,
And the wonderful grass upon your breast —
World, you are beautifully drest!

The wonderful air is over me,
And the wonderful wind is shaking the tree;
It walks on the water, and whirls the mills,
And talks to itself on the top of the hills.

You friendly Earth, how far do you go,
With the wheat-fields that nod and the rivers that flow,
With cities and gardens, and cliffs and isles,
And people upon you for thousands of miles?

Ah, you are so great, and I am so small,
I tremble to think of you, World, at all;
And yet, when I said my prayers to-day,
A whisper inside me seemed to say,
"You are more than the Earth, though you are such
        a dot:
You can love and think, and the Earth cannot."

PLAYTIME.

——o◦o◦o◦o——

TOPSY–TURVY WORLD.

" Lilliput Levee."

IF the butterfly courted the bee,
  And the owl the porcupine;
If churches were built in the sea,
  And three times one was nine;
If the pony rode his master;
  If the buttercups ate the cows;
If the cat had the dire disaster
  To be worried, sir, by the mouse;
If mamma, sir, sold the baby
  To a gypsy for half a crown;
If a gentleman, sir, was a lady,—
  The world would be Upside Down!
If any or all of these wonders
  Should ever come about,
I should not consider them blunders,
  For I should be Inside Out!

LITTLE MAMMA.

Charles Henry Webb.

Why is it the children don't love me
    As they do mamma?
That they put her ever above me —
    "Little mamma?"
I'm sure I do all that I can do.
What more can a rather big man do,
    Who can't be mamma —
        Little mamma?

Any game that the tyrants suggest,
"Logomachy," — which I detest, —
Doll-babies, hop-scotch, or base-ball,
I'm always on hand at the call.
When Noah and the others embark,
I'm the elephant saved in the ark.
I creep, and I climb, and I crawl —
By turns am the animals all.
        For the show on the stair
        I'm always the bear,
The chimpanzee, or the kangaroo.
        It is never "Mamma, —
            Little mamma, —
            Won't *you?*"

My umbrella's the pony, if any —
None ride on mamma's parasol;
I'm supposed to have always the penny
For bon-bons, and beggars, and all.

My room is the one where they clatter —
Am I reading, or writing, what matter!
My knee is the one for a trot,
My foot is the stirrup for Dot.
If his fractions get into a snarl
Who straightens the tangles for Karl?
Who bounds Massachusetts and Maine,
And tries to bound flimsy old Spain!
  Why,
   It is *I*,
    Papa, —
     Not little mamma!

That the youngsters are ingrates don't say.
I think they love me — in a way —
As one does the old clock on the stair, —
Any curious, cumbrous affair
That one's used to having about,
And would feel rather lonely without.
I think that they love me, I say,
In a sort of tolerant way;
   But it's plain that papa
    Isn't little mamma.

Thus when shadows come stealing anear,
And things in the firelight look queer;
When shadows the play-room enwrap,
They never climb into my lap
And toy with *my* head, smooth and bare,
As they do with mamma's shining hair;

Nor feel round my throat and my chin .
For dimples to put fingers in;
Nor lock my neck in a loving vise
And say they're "mousies" — that's mice —
  And will nibble my ears,
  Will nibble and bite
With their little mice-teeth, so sharp and so white,
If I do not kiss them this very minute —
Don't-wait-a-bit-but-at-once-begin-it. —
  Dear little papa!
  That's what they say and do to mamma.

If, mildly hinting, I quietly say that
Kissing's a game that more can play at,
They turn up at once those innocent eyes
And I suddenly learn to my great surprise
  That my face has "prickles" —
  My moustache tickles.
If storming their camp I seize a pert shaver,
And take as a right what was asked as a favor,
  It is, "O Papa,
  How horrid you are —
  You taste exactly like a cigar!"

But though the rebels protest and pout,
And make a pretence of driving me out,
I hold, after all, the main redoubt, —
Not by force of arms nor the force of will,
But the power of love, which is mightier still.
  And very deep in their hearts, I know,

Under the saucy and petulant " Oh,"
The doubtful " Yes," or the naughty " No,"
   They love papa.

And down in the heart that no one sees,
Where I hold my feasts and my jubilees,
I know that I would not abate one jot
Of the love that is held by my little Dot
Or my great big boy for their little mamma,
Though out in the cold it crowded papa.
I would not abate it the tiniest whit,
And I am not jealous the least little bit;
For I'll tell you a secret: Come, my dears,
And I'll whisper it — right-into-your-ears —
   I too love mamma,
     Little mamma!

WHERE'S MY BABY?

ANONYMOUS.

WHERE'S my baby? Where's my baby?
  But a little while ago,
In my arms I held one fondly.
  And a robe of lengthened flow
Covered little knees so dimpled
  And each pink and chubby toe.

Where's my baby? I remember
  Now about the shoes so red
Peeping from the shortened dresses,

And the first sweet words he said;
And the little teeth so pearly,
    And the bright curls on his head.

Where's my baby? In the door-yard
    Is a boy with shingled hair,
Whittling as he tries to whistle
    With a big boy's manly air,
With his trousers in his boot-tops,
    But my baby is not there.

Where's my baby? Where's my baby?
    Ah! the years fly on apace!
Yesterday I held and kissed it
    In its loveliness and grace;
But to-morrow sturdy manhood
    Takes the little baby's place.

LITTLE ORPHANT ANNIE.

JAMES WHITCOMB RILEY.

LITTLE Orphant Annie's come to our house to stay,
An' wash the cups an' saucers up, an' brush the crumbs
    away,
An' shoo the chickens off the porch, an' dust the
    hearth, an' sweep,
An' make the fire, an' bake the bread, an' earn her
    board-an'-keep;
An' all us other children, when the supper things is
    done,

We set around the kitchen fire an' has the mostest
    fun
A-list'nin' to the witch tales 'at Annie tells about,
An' the gobble-uns 'at gits you
           Ef you
             Don't
               Watch
                 Out!

Onc't they was a little boy wouldn't say his pray'rs —
An' when he went to bed 'at night, away up stairs,
His mammy heerd him holler, an' his daddy heerd him
    bawl,
An' when they turn't the kivvers down, he wasn't there
    at all!
An' they seeked him in the rafter-room, an' cubby-hole,
    an' press,
An' seeked him up the chimbly-flue, an' ever'wheres, I
    guess,
But all they ever found was thist his pants an' round-
    about!
An' the gobble-uns 'll git you
           Ef you
             Don't
               Watch
                 Out!

An' one time a little girl 'ud allus laugh an' grin,
An' make fun of ever' one an' all her blood-an'-kin,
An' onc't when they was " company," an' ole folks was
    there,

She mocked 'em an' shocked 'em, an' said she didn't
  care !
An' thist as she kicked her heels, an' turn't to run an'
  hide,
They was two great big Black Things a-standin' by her
  side,
An' they snatched her through the ceilin' 'fore she
  know'd what she's about !
An' the gobble-uns 'll git you
    Ef you
     Don't
      Watch
       Out !

An' little Orphant Annie says, when the blaze is blue,
An' the lampwick sputters, an the wind goes woo-oo !
An' you hear the crickets quit, an' the moon is gray,
An' the lightin'-bugs in dew is all squenched away —
You better mind yer parents, an' yer teachers fond an'
  dear,
An' churish them 'at loves you, an' dry the orphant's
  tear,
An' help the pore an' needy ones 'at clusters all about,
Er the gobble-uns 'll git you
    Ef you
     Don't
      Watch
       Out !

UNDER MY WINDOW.

Thomas B. Westwood.

Under my window, under my window,
　All in the midsummer weather,
Three little girls, with fluttering curls,
　Flit to and fro together: —
There's Bell with her bonnet of satin sheen,
And Maud with her mantle of silver-green,
　And Kate with her scarlet feather.

Under my window, under my window,
　Leaning stealthily over,
Merry and clear, the voice I hear
　Of each glad-hearted rover.
Ah! sly little Kate, she steals my roses,
And Maud and Bell twine wreaths and posies,
　As merry as bees in clover.

Under my window, under my window,
　In the blue midsummer weather,
Stealing slow, on a hushed tip-toe,
　I catch them all together: —
Bell with her bonnet of satin sheen,
And Maud with her mantle of silver-green,
　And Kate with the scarlet feather.

Under my window, under my window,
　And off through the orchard closes;
While Maud she flouts, and Bell she pouts,
　They scamper, and drop their posies;

But dear little Kate takes naught amiss,
And leaps in my arms with a loving kiss,
  And I give her all my roses.

WHAT ARE YOU GOOD FOR?

Emily Huntington Miller.

"What are you good for, my brave little man?
Answer that question for me if you can;
You, with your ringlets as bright as the sun,
You, with your fingers as white as a nun.
All the day long, with your busy contriving,
Into some mischief and fun you are driving.
See if your wise little noddle can tell
What you are good for, — now ponder it well."

Over the carpet the dear little feet
Came, with a patter, to climb on my seat;
Two little eyes, full of frolic and glee,
Under their lashes looked up unto me;
Two little hands, pressing close on my face,
Drew me down close, in a loving embrace;
Two little lips gave the answer so true,
"Good to love you, mamma, — good to love you!"

THE CHATTERBOX.

Jane Taylor.

From morning till night it was Lucy's delight
  To chatter and talk without stopping:

There was not a day but she rattled away,
  Like water forever a-dropping.

No matter at all if the subjects were small,
  Or not worth the trouble of saying,
'Twas equal to her, she would talking prefer
  To working, or reading, or playing.

You'll think now, perhaps, that there would have been
      gaps,
  If she had not been wonderful clever:
That her sense was so great, and so witty her pate,
  It would be forthcoming forever;

But that's quite absurd, for have you not heard
  That much tongue and few brains are connected?
That they are supposed to think least who talk most,
  And their wisdom is always suspected?

While Lucy was young, had she bridled her tongue,
  With a little good sense and exertion,
Who knows, but she might now have been our delight,
  Instead of our jest and aversion?

KEPT IN.

ETHEL LYNN BEERS.

"OH, jolly crow!
  You come and go —
You never ask permission;

Just look at me,
　Kept in — you see,
And fellers gone a-fishin'.

　"It's dull and hot
　In this old spot;
Outside, the wind is blowing,
　And — oh! that crook
　In meadow brook,
Where all the boys are going!

　"This 'Six times four'
　Is such a bore,
And so is 'Eight times seven.'
　I don't know why,
　The more I try,
The more I don't know ''leven.'

　"Old croaker, shoo!
　If I were you
I'd go to watch the fishin',
　And 'rithmetic
　Would vanish quick —
But what's the use of wishin'."

That solemn crow
　Looked high and low,
And paused a little season,
　Then answered, "Caws,
　You broke the laws
You suffer — that's the reason!"

And off he flew
The window through
By which he gained admission.
" Poor comfort this,
For sums amiss,
And boys gone off a-fishin' ! "

THE WOODEN DOLL AND THE WAX DOLL.

JANE TAYLOR.

THERE were two friends, a very charming pair !
Brunette the brown, and Blanchidine the fair ;
And she to love Brunette did constantly incline,
Nor less did Brunette love sweet Blanchidine.
Brunette in dress was neat, yet always plain ;
But Blanchidine of finery was vain.

Now Blanchidine a new acquaintance made —
A little girl most sumptuously arrayed,
In plumes and ribbons, gaudy to behold,
And India frock, with spots of shining gold.
Said Blanchidine, " A girl so richly dressed
Should surely be by every one caressed.
To play with me if she will condescend,
Henceforth 'tis she alone shall be my friend."
And so for this new friend in silks adorned,
Her poor Brunette was slighted, left, and scorned,

Of Blanchidine's vast stock of pretty toys,
A wooden doll her every thought employs ;

Its neck so white, so smooth, its cheeks so red —
She kiss'd, she fondled, and she took to bed.

Mamma now brought her home a doll of wax,
Its hair in ringlets white, as soft as flax ;
Its eyes could open and its eyes could shut;
And on it, too, with taste its clothes were put.
" My dear wax doll !" sweet Blanchidine would cry—
Her doll of wood was thrown neglected by.

One summer's day, — 'twas in the month of June, —
The sun blazed out in all the heat of noon :
"My waxen doll," she cried, " my dear, my charmer!
What, are you cold ? but you shall soon be warmer."
She laid it in the sun — misfortune dire !
The wax ran down as if before the fire !
Each beauteous feature quickly disappeared,
And melting, left a blank all soil'd and smeared.
Her doll disfigured she beheld amazed,
And thus expressed her sorrow as she gazed :
" Is it for you my heart I have estranged
From that I fondly loved, which has not changed ?
Just so may change my new acquaintance fine,
For whom I left Brunette, that friend of mine.

No more by outside show will I be lured :
Of such capricious whims I think I'm cured :
To plain old friends my heart shall still be true,
Nor change for every face because 'tis new."
Her slighted wooden doll resumed its charms,
And wrong'd Brunette she clasped within her arms.

THE OWL AND THE PUSSY-CAT.

Edward Lear.

The Owl and the Pussy-Cat went to sea
    In a beautiful pea-green boat;
They took some honey, and plenty of money
    Wrapped up in a five-pound note.
The Owl looked up to the moon above,
    And sang to a small guitar,
"O lovely Pussy! O Pussy, my love!
    What a beautiful Pussy you are, —
        You are,
    What a beautiful Pussy you are!"

Pussy said to the Owl, "You elegant fowl!
    How wonderful sweet you sing!
O let us be married, — too long we have tarried, —
    But what shall we do for a ring?"
They sailed away for a year and a day
    To the land where the Bong-tree grows,
And there in a wood, a piggy-wig stood
    With a ring in the end of his nose, —
        His nose,
    With a ring in the end of his nose.

"Dear Pig, are you willing to sell for one shilling
    Your ring?" Said the piggy, "I will."
So they took it away, and were married next day
    By the turkey who lives on the hill.

They dined upon mince and slices of quince,
  Which they ate with a runcible spoon,
And hand in hand on the edge of the sand
  They danced by the light of the moon, —
    The moon,
They danced by the light of the moon.

MEDDLESOME MATTY.

JANE TAYLOR.

ONE ugly trick has often spoiled
  The sweetest and the best;
Matilda, though a pleasant child,
  One ugly trick possessed,
Which, like a cloud before the skies,
Hid all her better qualities.

Sometimes she'd lift the tea-pot lid,
  To peep at what was in it;
Or tilt the kettle, if you did
  But turn your back a minute.
In vain you told her not to touch,
Her trick of meddling grew so much.

Her grandmamma went out one day,
  And by mistake she laid
Her spectacles and snuff-box gay
  Too near the little maid;
"Ah! well," thought she, "I'll try them on,
As soon as grandmamma is gone."

Forthwith she placed upon her nose
  The glasses large and wide ;
And looking round, as I suppose,
  The snuff-box too she spied :
" Oh ! what a pretty box is that ;
I'll open it," said little Matt.

" I know that grandmamma would say,
  ' Don't meddle with it, dear ' ;
But then, she's far enough away,
  And no one else is near :
Besides, what can there be amiss
In opening such a box as this ? "

So thumb and finger went to work
  To move the stubborn lid,
And presently a mighty jerk
  The mighty mischief did ;
For all at once, ah ! woful case,
The snuff came puffing in her face.

Poor eyes, and nose, and mouth beside
  A dismal sight presented ;
In vain, as bitterly she cried,
  Her folly she repented.
In vain she ran about for ease ;
She could do nothing now but sneeze.

She dash'd the spectacles away,
  To wipe her tingling eyes,
And as in twenty bits they lay,
  Her grandmamma she spies.

"Heyday! and what's the matter now?"
Says grandmamma with lifted brow.

Matilda, smarting with the pain,
    And tingling still, and sore,
Made many a promise to refrain
    From meddling evermore.
And 'tis a fact, as I have heard,
She ever since has kept her word.

A MODEST WIT.

SELLECK OSBORNE.

A SUPERCILIOUS nabob of the East —
    Haughty, being great — purse-proud, being rich —
A governor or general at the least,
    I have forgotten which —
Had in his family a humble youth
    Who went from England in his patron's suite,
An unassuming person, and in truth
    A lad of decent parts and good repute.

This youth had sense and spirit;
    But yet, with all his sense,
    Excessive diffidence
Obscured his merit.

One day, at table, flushed with pride and wine,
    His honor, proudly free, severely merry,

Conceived it would be vastly fine
  To crack a joke upon his secretary.

"Young man," he said, "by what art, craft, or trade
  Did your good father gain a livelihood?"
"He was a saddler, sir," Modestus said,
  "And in his time was reckoned good."

"A saddler, eh? and taught you Greek,
  Instead of teaching you to sew!
Pray, why did not your father make
  A saddler, sir, of you?"

Each parasite then, as in duty bound,
The joke applauded, and the laugh went round.
  At length Modestus, bowing low,
Said (craving pardon, if too free he made),
  "Sir, by your leave, I fain would know
Your father's trade."

"My father's trade! Come, come, sir! that's too bad!
My father's trade! Why, blockhead, are you mad?
My father, sir, did never stoop so low —
He was a gentleman, I'd have you know."

"Excuse the liberty I take,"
  Modestus said, with archness on his brow, —
"Pray, why did not your father make
  A gentleman of you?"

AN ELEGY ON THE DEATH OF A MAD DOG.

Oliver Goldsmith.

Good people all, of every sort,
  Give ear unto my song;
And if you find it wondrous short,
  It cannot hold you long.

In Islington there was a man,
  Of whom the world might say,
That still a godly race he ran
  Whene'er he went to pray.

A kind and gentle heart he had,
  To comfort friends and foes;
The naked every day he clad,
  When he put on his clothes.

And in that town a dog was found,
  As many dogs there be,
Both mongrel, puppy, whelp, and hound,
  And cur of low degree.

This dog and man at first were friends;
  But when a pique began,
The dog, to gain his private ends,
  Went mad, and bit the man.

Around from all the neighboring streets
  The wondering neighbors ran,
And swore the dog had lost his wits,
  To bite so good a man.

The wound it seemed both sore and sad
   To every Christian eye:
And while they swore the dog was mad,
   They swore the man would die.

But soon a wonder came to light,
   That showed the rogues they lied,
The man recovered of the bite,
   The dog it was that died.

A LAW–CASE.

WILLIAM COWPER.

BETWEEN Nose and Eyes a strange contest arose, —
   The spectacles set them unhappily wrong;
The point in dispute was, as all the world knows,
   To which the said spectacles ought to belong?

So Tongue was the lawyer, and argued the cause,
   With a great deal of skill, and a wig-full of learning,
While Chief-Justice Ear sat to balance the laws,
   So famed for his talent in nicely discerning.

" In behalf of the Nose it will quickly appear,
   And your Honor," he said, " will undoubtedly find,
That the Nose has had spectacles always in wear,
   Which amounts to possession, time out of mind."

Then, holding the spectacles up to the court,
   " Your Honor observes they are made with a straddle,

As wide as the ridge of the Nose is; in short,
   Designed to sit close to it, just like a saddle.

" Again, would your Honor a moment suppose
   ('Tis a case that has happened and may be again)
That the visage or countenance had not a nose,
   Pray who would, or who could, wear spectacles then ?

" On the whole it appears, and my argument shows,
   With a reasoning the court sure will never condemn,
That the spectacles plainly were made for the Nose,
   And the Nose was as plainly intended for them."

Then, shifting his side (as a lawyer knows how),
   He pleaded again in behalf of the Eyes;
But what were his arguments few people know,
   For the court did not think they were equally wise.

So his Honor decreed, with a grave, solemn tone,
   Decisive and clear, without one *if* or *but*,
That, whenever the Nose put his spectacles on
   By daylight or candle-light, Eyes should be shut.

THE JOVIAL BEGGAR.

OLD SONG.

THERE was a jovial beggar,
   He had a wooden leg,
Lame from his cradle,
   And forced for to beg.

And a-begging we will go,
    Will go, will go,
And a-begging we will go.

A bag for his oatmeal,
    Another for his salt,
And a long pair of crutches,
    To show that he can halt.
And a-begging we will go,
    Will go, will go,
And a-begging we will go.

A bag for his wheat,
    Another for his rye,
And a little bottle by his side,
    To drink when he's a-dry.
And a-begging we will go,
    Will go, will go,
And a-begging we will go.

Seven years I begg'd
    For my old master Wilde,
He taught me how to beg
    When I was but a child.
And a-begging we will go,
    Will go, will go,
And a-begging we will go.

I begged for my master,
    And got him store of pelf,
But goodness now be praised,
    I'm begging for myself.

And a-begging we will go,
        Will go, will go,
And a-begging we will go.

In a hollow tree
    I live, and pay no rent,
Providence provides for me,
    And I am well content.
And a-begging we will go,
        Will go, will go,
And a-begging we will go.

Of all the occupations
    A beggar's is the best,
For whenever he's a-weary,
    He can lay him down to rest,
And a-begging we will go,
        Will go, will go,
And a-begging we will go.

I fear no plots against me,
    I live in open cell:
Then who would be a king, lads,
    When the beggar lives so well?
And a-begging we will go,
        Will go, will go,
And a-begging we will go.

THE PIED PIPER OF HAMELIN.

ROBERT BROWNING.

HAMELIN Town's in Brunswick,
By famous Hanover city;
  The river Weser, deep and wide,
  Washes its wall on the southern side;
  A pleasanter spot you never spied;
But when begins my ditty,
  Almost five hundred years ago,
  To see the townsfolk suffer so
From vermin, was a pity.

   Rats!
They fought the dogs, and killed the cats,
  And bit the babies in the cradles,
And ate the cheeses out of the vats,
  And licked the soup from the cook's own ladles,
Split open the kegs of salted sprats,
Made nests inside men's Sunday hats.
And even spoiled the women's chats,
  By drowning their speaking
  With shrieking and squeaking
In fifty different sharps and flats.

At last the people in a body
  To the Town Hall came flocking:
"'Tis clear," cried they, "our Mayor's a noddy;
  And as for our Corporation — shocking
To think we buy gowns lined with ermine

For dolts that can't or won't determine
What's best to rid us of our vermin!
You hope, because your're old and obese,
To find in the furry civic robe ease?
Rouse up, sirs! Give your brains a racking
To find the remedy we're lacking,
Or, sure as fate, we'll send you packing!"
At this the Mayor and Corporation
Quaked with a mighty consternation.

An hour they sate in counsel —
    At length the Mayor broke silence :
" For a guilder I'd my ermine gown sell;
I wish I were a mile hence!
It's easy to bid one rack one's brain —
I'm sure my poor head aches again,
I've scratched it so, and all in vain.
Oh for a trap, a trap, a trap!"
Just as he said this, what should hap
At the chamber door but a gentle tap?
" Bless us," cried the Mayor, " what's that?"
(With the Corporation as he sat,
Looking little though wondrous fat,
Nor brighter was his eye, nor moister
Than a too-long-opened oyster,
Save when at noon his paunch grew mutinous
For a plate of turtle, green and glutinous,)
" Only a scraping of shoes on the mat?
Anything like the sound of a rat
Makes my heart go pit-a-pat!"

" Come in ! " the Mayor cried, looking bigger ;
And in did come the strangest figure :
His queer long coat from heel to head
Was half of yellow and half of red ;
And he himself was tall and thin ;
With sharp blue eyes, each like a pin ;
And light, loose hair, yet swarthy skin ;
No tuft on cheek nor beard on chin,
But lips where smiles went out and in —
There was no guessing his kith and kin ;
And nobody could enough admire
The tall man and his quaint attire.
Quoth one, " It's as my great-grandsire,
Starting up at the trump of doom's tone,
Had walked this way from his painted tombstone ! "

He advanced to the council-table :
And, " Please your honors," said he, " I'm able,
By means of a secret charm, to draw
All creatures living beneath the sun,
That creep, or swim, or fly, or run,
After me so as you never saw !
And I chiefly use my charm
On creatures that do people harm —
The mole, and toad, and newt, and viper —
And people call me the Pied Piper."

(And here they noticed round his neck
    A scarf of red and yellow stripe,
To match with his coat of the self-same check ;
    And at the scarf's end hung a pipe ;

And his fingers, they noticed, were ever straying
As if impatient to be playing
Upon this pipe, as low it dangled
Over his vesture so old-fangled.)
"Yet," said he, "poor piper as I am,
In Tartary I freed the Cham,
Last June, from his huge swarm of gnats;
I eased in Asia the Nizam
Of a monstrous brood of vampire-bats;
And, as for what your brain bewilders —
If I can rid your town of rats,
Will you give me a thousand guilders?"
"One? fifty thousand!" — was the exclamation
Of the astonished Mayor and Corporation.

Into the street the Piper stept,
    Smiling first a little smile,
As if he knew what magic slept
    In his quiet pipe the while;
Then, like a musical adept,
To blow the pipe his lips he wrinkled,
And green and blue his sharp eyes twinkled,
Like a candle flame where salt is sprinkled;
And ere three shrill notes the pipe uttered,
You heard as if an army muttered;
And the muttering grew to a grumbling;
And the grumbling grew to a mighty rumbling;
And out of the houses the rats came tumbling.
Great rats, small rats, lean rats, brawny rats,
Brown rats, black rats, gray rats, tawny rats,

Grave old plodders, gay young friskers,
    Fathers, mothers, uncles, cousins,
Cocking tails and pricking whiskers;
    Families by tens and dozens,
Brothers, sisters, husbands, wives —
Followed the Piper for their lives.
From street to street he piped advancing,
And step for step they followed dancing,
Until they came to the river Weser,
Wherein all plunged and perished,
    Save one who, stout as Julius Cæsar,
Swam across and lived to carry
(As he the manuscript he cherished)
To rat-land home his commentary,
Which was: "At the first shrill notes of the pipe,
I heard a sound as of scraping tripe,
And putting apples, wondrous ripe,
Into a cider-press's gripe —
And a moving away of pickle-tub-boards,
And a leaving ajar of conserve-cupboards,
And a drawing the corks of train-oil flasks,
And breaking the hoops of butter-casks;
And it seemed as if a voice
(Sweeter far than by harp or by psaltery
Is breathed) call out, O rats, rejoice!
The world is grown to one vast drysaltery!
So munch on, crunch on, take your nuncheon,
Breakfast, supper, dinner, luncheon!
And just as a bulky sugar-puncheon,
All ready staved, like a great sun shone

Glorious, scarce an inch before me,
Just as me thought it said, Come, bore me!
—I found the Weser rolling o'er me."
You should have heard the Hamelin people
Ringing the bells till they rocked the steeple;
"Go," cried the Mayor, "and get long poles!
Poke out the nests and block up the holes!
Consult with carpenters and builders,
And leave in our town not even a trace
Of the rats!"—when suddenly, up the face
Of the Piper perked in the market-place,
With a "First, if you please, my thousand guilders!"
A thousand guilders! The Mayor looked blue!
So did the Corporation too.
For council dinners make rare havoc
With Claret, Moselle, Vin-de-Grave, Hock:
And half the money would replenish
Their cellar's biggest butt with Rhenish.
To pay this sum to a wandering fellow
With a gypsy coat of red and yellow!
"Beside," quoth the Mayor, with a knowing wink,
"Our business was done at the river's brink;
We saw with our eyes the vermin sink,
And what's dead can't come to life, I think.
So, friend, we're not the folks to shrink
From the duty of giving you something for drink,
And a matter of money to put in your poke;
But, as for the guilders, what we spoke
Of them, as you very well know, was in joke;
Beside, our losses have made us thrifty;
A thousand guilders! Come, take fifty!"

The Piper's face fell, and he cried,
"No trifling! I can't wait! beside,
I've promised to visit by dinner-time
Bagdat, and accept the prime
Of the head cook's pottage, all he's rich in,
For having left, in the Caliph's kitchen,
Of a nest of scorpions no survivor —
With him I proved no bargain-driver,
With you, don't think I'll bate a stiver!
And folks who put me in a passion
May find me pipe to another fashion."
"How?" cried the Mayor, "d'ye think I'll brook
Being worse treated than a cook?
Insulted by a lazy ribald
With idle pipe and vesture piebald?
You threaten us, fellow? Do your worst,
Blow your pipe there till you burst!"

Once more he stept into the street;
And to his lips again
Laid his long pipe of smooth straight cane;
And ere he blew three notes (such sweet
Soft notes as yet musician's cunning
    Never gave the enraptured air)
There was a rustling that seemed like a bustling
Of merry crowds justling at pitching and hustling;
Small feet were pattering, wooden shoes clattering,
Little hands clapping, and little tongues chattering,
And, like fowls in a farm-yard when barley is scatter-
        ing,
Out came the children running:

All the little boys and girls,
With rosy cheeks and flaxen curls,
And sparkling eyes and teeth like pearls,
Tripping and skipping, ran merrily after
The wonderful music with shouting and laughter.

The Mayor was dumb, and the Council stood
As if they were changed into blocks of wood.
Unable to move a step, or cry
To the children merrily skipping by —
And could only follow with the eye
That joyous crowd at the Piper's back.
But how the Mayor was on the rack,
And the wretched Council's bosoms beat,
As the Piper turned from the High Street
To where the Weser rolled its waters
Right in the way of their sons and daughters!
However, he turned from south to west,
And to Koppelberg Hill his steps addressed,
And after him the children pressed;
Great was the joy in every breast.

" He never can cross that mighty top!
He's forced to let the piping drop,
And we shall see our children stop!"
When, lo, as they reached the mountain's side,
A wondrous portal opened wide,
As if a cavern was suddenly hollowed;
And the Piper advanced and the children followed;
And when all were in, to the very last,
The door in the mountain-side shut fast.

Did I say all? No! One was lame,
And could not dance the whole of the way;
And in after-years, if you would blame
His sadness, he was used to say, —
"It's dull in our town since my playmates left!
I can't forget that I'm bereft
Of all the pleasant sights they see,
Which the Piper also promised me;
For he led us, he said, to a joyous land,
Joining the town and just at hand,
Where waters gushed and fruit-trees grew,
And flowers put forth of a fairer hue,
And every thing was strange and new;
The sparrows were brighter than peacocks here,
And their dogs outran our fallow deer,
And honey-bees had lost their stings,
And horses were born with eagles' wings;
And just as I became assured
My lame foot would be speedily cured,
The music stopped and I stood still,
And found myself outside the Hill,
Left alone against my will.
To go now limping as before,
And never hear of that country more!"

Alas, alas for Hamelin!
    There came into many a burgher's pate
    A text which says, that Heaven's gate
    Opes to the rich at as easy rate
As the needle's eye takes a camel in!

The Mayor sent East, West, North and South,
To offer the Piper by word of mouth,
   Wherever it was men's lot to find him,
Silver and gold to his heart's content,
If he'd only return the way he went,
   And bring the children behind him.
But when they saw 'twas a lost endeavor,
And piper and dancers were gone forever,
They made a decree that lawyers never
   Should think their records dated duly
If, after the day of the month and year,
These words did not as well appear,
" And so long after what happened here
   On the twenty-second of July,
Thirteen Hundred and Seventy-six : "
And the better in memory to fix
The place of the children's last retreat
They called it the Pied Piper's Street —
Where any one playing on pipe or tabor
Was sure for the future to lose his labor.
Nor suffered they hostelry or tavern
To shock with mirth a street so solemn ;
But opposite the place of the cavern
   They wrote the story on a column,
And on the Great Church window painted
The same, to make the world acquainted
How their children were stolen away ;
And there it stands to this very day.
And I must not omit to say
That in Transylvania there's a tribe

Of alien people that ascribe
The outlandish ways and dress
On which their neighbors lay such stress
To their fathers and mothers having risen
Out of some subterranean prison
Into which they were trepanned
Long time ago, in a mighty band,
Out of Hamelin town in Brunswick land,
But how or why, they don't understand.

So, Willy, let you and me be wipers
Of scores out with all men — especially pipers;
And, whether they pipe us free from rats or from
        mice,
If we've promised them aught, let us keep our promise.

MEMORY RHYMES.

THE SEVEN WONDERS OF THE WORLD.

The Editors.

At Alexandria's water-gate
    Her lighted *Pharos* shone.
The *Hanging Gardens'* magic green
    Delighted Babylon.

The great *Colossus* stretched his limbs
 Across the Rhodian straits.
Diana's mighty *Temple* rose
 Within the Ephesian gates.
Halicarnassus held the *Tomb*
 Of haughty king and queen;
The famous mazy *Labyrinth*
 In ancient Crete was seen.
The *Pyramid* its mighty foot
 Plants in Egyptian sands,
And this alone of all the seven,
 To-day unruined stands.

THE NINE MUSES.

THE EDITORS.

HERE the sisters nine we see,
Born of divine *Mnemosyne:*
Terpsichore in graceful dance,
Melpomene with tragic glance,
Euterpe with the lyric cry,
And *Erato* with lover's sigh.
Thalia leads the comic throng;
And *Polyhymnia,* sacred song.
Urania sings of starry hosts;
Calliope her heroes boasts.
Clio, on tablets and on scrolls,
 The history of the world enrolls.
Mt. Helicon is their abode;
The first to name them, *Hesiod.*

SIGNS OF THE ZODIAC.

ANONYMOUS.

THE *Ram*, the *Bull*, the *Heavenly Twins*,
The *Crab* who near the *Lion* shines,
    The *Virgin* and the *Scales ;*
The *Scorpion*, *Archer*, and *He-Goat*,
The man who bears the *Watering-pot*,
    And *Fish* with glittering tails.

THE CALENDAR.

ANONYMOUS.

THIRTY days hath September,
April, June, and November;
All the rest have thirty-one,
Excepting February alone,
Which hath but twenty-eight in fine,
Till leap-year gives it twenty-nine.

TABLE RULES FOR LITTLE FOLKS.

ANONYMOUS.

IN silence I must take my seat,
And give God thanks. before I eat;
Must for my food in patience wait,
Till I am asked to hand my plate.
I must not scold, nor whine, nor pout,

Nor move my chair or plate about;
With knife or fork or anything,
I must not play; nor must I sing.
I must not speak a useless word,
For children should be seen — not heard;
I must not talk about my food,
Nor fret if I don't think it good.
I must not say, " the bread is old, —
The tea is hot, — the coffee's cold ";
I must not cry for this or that,
Nor murmur if my meat is fat.
My mouth with food I must not crowd,
Nor while I'm eating speak aloud;
Must turn my head to cough or sneeze.
And when I ask say, " If you please."
The table-cloth I must not spoil,
Nor with my food my fingers soil;
Must keep my seat when I have done,
Nor round the table sport or run.
When told to rise, then I must put
My chair away with noiseless foot;
And lift my heart to God above,
In praise for all His wondrous love.

LOYALTY.

HEROISM.

FIFE AND DRUM.

STATUE OF ST. GEORGE. DONATELLO.

LOYALTY AND HEROISM.

GOING HOME.

N. P. WILLIS.

BRIGHT flag at yonder tapering mast,
    Fling out your field of azure blue;
Let star and stripe be westward cast,
    And point as Freedom's eagle flew!
Strain home! O lithe and quivering spars!
Point home, my country's flag of stars!

NATIONAL HYMN.

SAMUEL F. SMITH.

MY country, 'tis of thee,
Sweet land of liberty,
    Of thee I sing;
Land where my fathers died,
Land of the pilgrim's pride,
From every mountain side
    Let freedom ring.

My native country, thee —
Land of the noble free —
   Thy name I love;
I love thy rocks and rills,
Thy woods and templed hills;
My heart with rapture thrills
   Like that above.

Let music swell the breeze,
And ring from all the trees
   Sweet freedom's song;
Let mortal tongues awake;
Let all that breathe partake;
Let rocks their silence break —
   The sound prolong.

Our fathers' God, to thee,
Author of liberty,
   To thee we sing:
Long may our land be bright
With freedom's holy light;
Protect us by thy might,
   Great God, our King.

MY NATIVE LAND.

WALTER SCOTT.

BREATHES there the man with soul so dead,
Who never to himself hath said,
   "This is my own — my native land!"

Whose heart hath ne'er within him burned,
As home his footsteps he hath turned,
　From wandering on a foreign strand?
If such there breathe, go, mark him well!
For him no minstrel's raptures swell.
High though his titles, proud his name,
Boundless his wealth as wish can claim, —
Despite those titles, power, and pelf,
The wretch, concentered all in self,
Living shall forfeit fair renown,
And, doubly dying, shall go down
To the vile dust from whence he sprung,
Unwept, unhonored, and unsung.

THE AMERICAN FLAG.

JOSEPH RODMAN DRAKE.　EXTRACT.

WHEN Freedom from her mountain height
　Unfurled her standard to the air,
She tore the azure robe of night,
　And set the stars of glory there.
She mingled with its gorgeous dyes
The milky baldric of the skies,
And striped its pure, celestial white,
With streakings of the morning light;
Then from his mansion in the sun
She called her eagle bearer down,
And gave into his mighty hand
The symbol of her chosen land.

THE SEMINOLE'S DEFIANCE.

G. W. PATTEN.

BLAZE, with your serried columns! I will not bend
    the knee;
The shackle ne'er again shall bind the arm which now
    is free!
I've mailed it with the thunder, when the tempest
    muttered low;
And where it falls, ye well may dread the lightning
    of its blow.
I've scared you in the city; I've scalped you on the plain;
Go, count your chosen where they fell beneath my
    leaden rain!
I scorn your proffered treaty; the pale-face I defy;
Revenge is stamped upon my spear, and "blood" my
    battle-cry!

Some strike for hope of booty; some to defend their
    all;—
I battle for the joy I have to see the white man fall.
I love, among the wounded, to hear his dying moan,
And catch, while chanting at his side, the music of his
    groan.
Ye've trailed me through the forest; ye've tracked me
    o'er the stream;
And struggling through the everglade your bristling
    bayonets gleam.
But I stand as should the warrior, with his rifle and
    his spear;

The scalp of vengeance still is red, and warns you, —
  "Come not here!"

Think ye to find my homestead? — I gave it to the fire.
My tawny household do you seek? — I am a childless
  sire.
But, should ye crave life's nourishment, enough I have
  and good;
I live on hate, — 'tis all my bread; yet light is not my
  food.
I loathe you with my bosom! I scorn you with mine
  eye!
And I'll taunt you with my latest breath, and fight you
  till I die!
I ne'er will ask for quarter, and I ne'er will be your
  slave;
But I'll swim the sea of slaughter till I sink beneath
  the wave!

THE BIVOUAC OF THE DEAD.

THEODORE O'HARA. EXTRACT.

THE muffled drum's sad roll has beat
  The soldier's last tattoo;
No more on life's parade shall meet
  That brave and fallen few.
On Fame's eternal camping-ground
  Their silent tents are spread,
And glory guards with solemn round
  The bivouac of the dead.

LORRAINE.

CHARLES KINGSLEY.

"ARE you ready for your steeple-chase, Lorraine, Lor-
    raine, Lorrèe ?
Barum, Barum, Barum, Barum, Barum, Barum, Baree.
You're booked to ride your capping race to-day at Coul-
    terlee,
You're booked to ride Vindictive, for all the world to see,
To keep him straight, and keep him first, and win the
    run for me."
Barum, Barum, Barum, Barum, Barum, Barum, Baree.

She clasped her new-born baby, poor Lorraine, Lorraine,
    Lorrèe,
Barum, Barum, Barum, Barum, Barum, Barum, Baree.
"I cannot ride Vindictive, as any man might see,
And I will not ride Vindictive, with this baby on my
    knee,
He's killed a boy, he's killed a man, and why should
    he kill me ?"

"Unless you ride Vindictive, Lorraine, Lorraine, Lorrèe,
Unless you ride Vindictive, to-day at Coulterlee,
And land him safe across the brook, and win the blank
    for me,
It's you may keep your baby, for you'll get no keep
    from me."

"That husbands could be cruel," said Lorraine, Lor-
    raine, Lorrèe,

" That husbands could be cruel, I have known for sea-
  sons three ;
But oh! to ride Vindictive, while a baby cries for me,
And be killed across a fence at last for all the world
  to see ! "

She mastered young Vindictive, — oh! the gallant lass
  was she !
And kept him straight, and won the race, as near as
  near could be ;
But he killed her at the brook against a pollard willow
  tree,
Oh, he killed her at the brook, the brute, for all the
  world to see, —
And no one but the baby cried for poor Lorraine, Lorrèe.

HEROES.

ANONYMOUS.

THE wind was soft and heavy,
  Where African palm-trees tower,
Hardly stirring the river,
  Hardly shaking a flower;
The night was grave and splendid,
  A dead queen lying in state,
With all her jewels upon her,
  And trumpets at her gate.

The wild notes waved and linger'd,
  And fainted along the air,

Sometimes like defiance,
   And sometimes like despair;
When down the moonlit mountain,
   And beside the river-calms,
The line of a dismal procession
   Unwound between the palms.

A train of driven captives,
   Weary, weak, amazed, —
Eighty hopeless faces,
   Never once upraised;
Bleeding from the journey,
   Longing for the grave:
Men, and women, and children,
   Every one a slave.

Lashed, and crying, and crouching,
   They pass'd, suspecting not
There were three or four English
   Whose hearts grew very hot, —
Men who had come from a distance,
   Whose lives were in their hands,
To tell the love of Jesus
   Among the heathen lands;

Studious men and gentle,
   But not in the least afraid:
With fire enough amongst them
   To furnish a crusade.
And when they saw the slave-troop
   Come hurrying down the hill,

Each man look'd at the other,
  Unable to be still.

They did not care for treaties,
  And death they did not fear;
One great wrong would have roused them, —
  There were eighty here.
They were not doing man's work,
  They were doing the Lord's,
So they went and stopp'd the savages
  With these amazing words: —

" We are three or four English,
  And we CANNOT LET THIS BE, —
Get away to your mountains,
  And set the people free!"
You should have seen the black men,
  How gray their faces turn;
They think the name of England
  Is something that will burn.

They break, they fly like water
  In a rushing, mighty wind;
The slaves stretch out uncertain hands,
  By long despair made blind,
Till in a wonderful moment
  The gasp of freedom came,
Like the leap of a tropical sunrise,
  That sets the world aflame.

A blast of weeping and shouting
  Cleansed all the guilty place;

And God was able to undraw
   The curtain from His Face.
A hundred years of preaching
   Could not proclaim the creed
Of Love, and Power, and Pity
   So well as that one deed.

A glorious gift is Prudence;
   And they are useful friends
Who never make beginnings
   Till they can see the ends;
But give us now and then a man,
   That we may make him king,
Just to scorn the consequence,
   And just to DO THE THING.

FIGHTING.

THOMAS HUGHES. ARRANGED.

Boys will quarrel, and when they quarrel will sometimes fight. Learn to box, then, as you learn to play cricket and football. Not one of you will be the worse but very much the better for learning to box well. Should you never have to use it in earnest, there's no exercise in the world so good for the temper and for the muscles of the back and legs.

As to fighting, keep out of it if you can, by all means. When the time comes, if it ever should, that you have to say "Yes" or "No" to a challenge to fight, say

"No" if you can,—only take care you make it clear to yourselves why you say "No." It's a proof of the highest courage if done from true Christian motives. It's quite right and justifiable, if done from a simple aversion to physical pain and danger. But don't say "No" because you fear a licking, and say or think it's because you fear God, for that's neither Christian nor honest. And if you do fight, fight it out; and don't give in while you can stand and see.

CASABIANCA.

FELICIA HEMANS.

THE boy stood on the burning deck,
    Whence all but him had fled;
The flame that lit the battle's wreck,
    Shone round him o'er the dead.

Yet beautiful and bright he stood,
    As born to rule the storm;
A creature of heroic blood,
    A proud, though child-like form.

The flames roll'd on—he would not go
    Without his father's word;
That father, faint in death below,
    His voice no longer heard.

He call'd aloud—"Say, father, say
    If yet my task is done?"

He knew not that the chieftain lay
  Unconscious of his son.

"Speak, father!" once again he cried,
  "If I may yet be gone!"
— And but the booming shots replied,
  And fast the flames roll'd on.

Upon his brow he felt their breath,
  And in his waving hair;
And look'd from that lone post of death,
  In still, yet brave despair.

And shouted but once more aloud,
  "My father! must I stay?"
While o'er him fast, through sail and shroud,
  The wreathing fires made way.

They wrapt the ship in splendor wild,
  They caught the flag on high,
And stream'd above the gallant child,
  Like banners in the sky.

There came a burst of thunder sound —
  The boy — oh! where was he!
— Ask of the winds that far around
  With fragments strew'd the sea!

With mast, and helm, and pennon fair,
  That well had borne their part —
But the noblest thing that perish'd there,
  Was that young faithful heart.

HOME.

Alfred Tennyson.

Home they brought him, slain with spears,
  They brought him home at even-fall;
All alone she sits and hears
    Echoes in his empty hall,
      Sounding on the morrow.

The sun peep'd in from open field,
  The boy began to leap and prance,
  Rode upon his father's lance,
Beat upon his father's shield —
    "O hush, my joy, my sorrow."

SOLDIER, REST!

Walter Scott.   Song from "The Lady of the Lake."

Soldier, rest! thy warfare o'er,
  Sleep the sleep that knows not breaking;
Dream of battle-fields no more,
  Days of danger, nights of waking.
In our isle's enchanted hall,
  Hands unseen thy couch are strewing;
Fairy strains of music fall,
  Every sense in slumber dewing.
Soldier, rest! thy warfare o'er,
Dream of fighting fields no more;

Sleep the sleep that knows not breaking,
Morn of toil, nor night of waking.

No rude sound shall reach thine ear,
    Armor's clang, or war-steed's champing,
Trump nor pibroch summon here,
    Mustering clan, or squadron tramping.
Yet the lark's shrill fife may come,
    At the day-break, from the fallow,
And the bittern sound his drum,
    Booming from the sedgy shallow.
Ruder sounds shall none be near,
Guard's nor warder's challenge here,
Here's no war-steed's neigh and champing,
Shouting clans, or squadrons stamping.

Huntsman, rest! thy chase is done,
    While our slumb'rous spells assail ye,
Dream not with the rising sun,
    Bugles here shall sound reveillé.
Sleep! the deer is in his den;
    Sleep! thy hounds are by thee lying;
Sleep! nor dream, in yonder glen,
    How thy gallant steed lay dying.
Huntsman, rest! thy chase is done,
Think not of the rising sun,
For at dawning to assail ye,
Here no bugles sound reveillé.

SONG OF MARION'S MEN.

WILLIAM CULLEN BRYANT.

OUR band is few but true and tried,
  Our leader frank and bold,
The British soldier trembles
  When Marion's name is told.
Our fortress is the good greenwood,
  Our tent the cypress tree,
We know the forest round us,
  As seamen know the sea.
We know its vales of thorny vines,
  Its glades of reedy grass,
Its safe and silent islands
  Within the dark morass.

Woe to the English soldiery,
  That little dream us near!
On them shall light at midnight
  A strange and sudden fear,
When, waking to their tents on fire,
  They grasp their arms in vain;
And they who stand to face us
  Are beat to earth again,
And they who fly in terror, dream
  A mighty host behind,
And hear the tramp of thousands
  Upon the hollow wind.

Then sweet the hour that brings release
  From danger and from toil;

We talk the battle over,
   And share the battle spoil.
The woodland rings with laugh and shout,
   As if a hunt were up,
And woodland flowers are gathered
   To crown the soldier's cup.
With merry songs we mock the wind
   That in the pine-top grieves,
And slumber long and sweetly
   On beds of oaken leaves.

Well knows the fair and friendly moon
   The band that Marion leads —
The glitter of their rifles,
   The scampering of their steeds.
'Tis life to guide the fiery barb
   Across the moonlit plain;
'Tis life to feel the night-wind
   That lifts his tossing mane.
A moment in the British camp,
   A moment — and away!
Back to the pathless forest
   Before the peep of day.

Grave men there are by broad Santee,
   Grave men with hoary hairs;
Their hearts are all with Marion,
   For Marion are their prayers.
And lovely ladies greet our band
   With kindliest welcoming,

With smiles like those of summer,
　And tears like those of spring.
For them we wear these trusty arms,
　And lay them down no more,
Till we have driven the Briton
　Forever from our shore!

BANNOCKBURN.

Robert Burns.

Scots, wha hae wi' Wallace bled,
Scots, wham Bruce has aften led;
Welcome to your gory bed,
　　Or to victorie.

Now's the day, and now's the hour;
See the front o' battle lower;
See approach proud Edward's power —
　　Chains and slaverie!

Wha will be a traitor knave?
Wha can fill a coward's grave?
Wha sae base as be a slave?
　　Let him turn and flee!

Wha for Scotland's king and law
Freedom's sword will strongly draw,
Freeman stand, or freeman fa'?
　　Let him on wi' me!

By oppression's woes and pains!
By your sons in servile chains!
We will drain our dearest veins,
     But they *shall* be free!

Lay the proud usurpers low!
Tyrants fall in every foe!
Liberty's in every blow!
     Let us do, or die!

ANDREW HOFER.

JULIUS MOSEN.

AT Mantua in chains
   The gallant Hofer lay,
In Mantua to death
   Led him the foe away;
His brothers' hearts bled for the chief,
For Germany disgrace and grief
   And Tyrol's mountain-land!

His hands behind him clasped,
   With firm and measured pace,
Marched Andrew Hofer on;
   He feared not death to face,
Death whom from Iselberg aloft
Into the vale he sent so oft,
   In Tyrol's holy land.

But when from dungeon-grate,
   In Mantua's stronghold,

Their hands on high he saw
   His faithful brothers hold,
"O God be with you all!" he said,
"And with the German realm betrayed,
   And Tyrol's holy land!"

The drummer's hand refused
   To beat the solemn march,
While Andrew Hofer passed
   The portal's gloomy arch;
In fetters shackled, yet so free,
There on the bastion stood he,
   Brave Tyrol's gallant son.

They bade him then kneel down,
   He answered, "I will not!
Here standing will I die,
   As I have stood and fought,
As now I tread this bulwark's bank,
Long life to my good Kaiser Frank,
   And, Tyrol, hail to thee!"

A grenadier then took
   The bandage from his hand,
While Hofer spake a prayer,
   His last on earthly land.
"Mark well!" he with loud voice exclaimed,
"Now fire! Ah! 'twas badly aimed!
   O Tyrol, fare thee well!"

THE MINSTREL–BOY.

THOMAS MOORE.

THE Minstrel-boy to the war is gone,
  In the ranks of death you'll find him;
His father's sword he has girded on,
  And his wild harp slung behind him. —
"Land of song!" said the warrior bard,
  "Though all the world betrays thee,
One sword, at least, thy right shall guard,
  One faithful harp shall praise thee!"

The Minstrel fell! — but the foeman's chain
  Could not bring his proud soul under:
The harp he loved ne'er spoke again,
  For he tore its chords asunder;
And said, "No chain shall sully thee,
  Thou soul of love and bravery!
Thy songs were made for the brave and free, —
  They shall never sound in slavery!"

BEFORE SEDAN.

AUSTIN DOBSON.

HERE in this leafy place
  Quiet he lies,
Cold, with his sightless face
  Turned to the skies;
'Tis but another dead;
All you can say is said.

Carry his body hence, —
  Kings must have slaves;
Kings climb to eminence
  Over men's graves;
So this man's eyes are dim; —
Throw the earth over him.

What was the white you touched
  There at his side?
Paper his hand had clutched
  Tight ere he died; —
Message or wish, may be; —
Smooth the folds out and see.

Hardly the worst of us
  Here could have smiled! —
Only the tremulous
  Words of a child; —
Prattle, that has for stops
Just a few ruddy drops.

Look. She is sad to miss,
  Morning and night,
His — her dead father's — kiss,
  Tries to be bright,
Good to mamma, and sweet;
That is all. " Marguerite."

Ah, if beside the dead
  Slumbered the pain!

Ah, if the hearts that bled
  Slept with the slain!
If the grief died; — but no; —
Death will not have it so.

THE CHARGE OF THE LIGHT BRIGADE.

ALFRED TENNYSON.

HALF a league, half a league,
Half a league onward,
All in the valley of death
Rode the six hundred.
"Forward, the Light Brigade!
Take the guns!" Nolan said;
Into the valley of Death
  Rode the six hundred.

"Forward, the Light Brigade!"
Was there a man dismayed?
Not though the soldier knew
  Some one had blundered;
Theirs not to make reply,
Theirs not to reason why,
Theirs but to do and die; —
Into the valley of Death
  Rode the six hundred.

Cannon to right of them,
Cannon to left of them,

Cannon in front of them
   Volleyed and thundered.
Stormed at with shot and shell,
Boldly they rode and well;
Into the jaws of Death,
Into the mouth of Hell
   Rode the six hundred.

Flashed all their sabres bare,
Flashed as they turned in air,
Sabring the gunners there,
Charging an army, while
   All the world wondered.
Plunged in the battery smoke,
Right through the line they broke;
Cossack and Russian
Reeled from the sabre-stroke —
   Shattered and sundered.
Then they rode back, but not —
   Not the six hundred.

Cannon to right of them,
Cannon to left of them,
Cannon behind them
   Volleyed and thundered.
Stormed at with shot and shell,
While horse and hero fell,
Those that had fought so well
Came through the jaws of Death,
Back from the mouth of Hell,

All that was left of them,
　　Left of six hundred.

When can their glory fade?
Oh, the wild charge they made!
　　All the world wondered.
Honor the charge they made!
Honor the Light Brigade!
　　Noble six hundred.

WARREN'S ADDRESS.

JOHN PIERPONT.

STAND! the ground's your own, my braves!
Will ye give it up to slaves?
Will ye look for greener graves?
　　Hope ye mercy still?
What's the mercy despots feel?
Hear it in that battle peal!
Read it on yon bristling steel!
　　Ask it ye who will!

Fear ye foes who kill for hire?
Will ye to your homes retire?
Look behind you! they're afire,
　　And, before you, see
Who have done it! From the vale
On they come! and will ye quail?

Leaden rain and leaden hail
  Let their welcome be!

In the God of battles trust!
Die we may — and die we must;
But oh, where can dust to dust
  Be consigned so well,
As where heaven its dews shall shed
On the martyred patriot's bed,
And the rocks shall raise their head
  Of his deeds to tell!

THE NORMAN BATTLE–SONG.

ANONYMOUS.

Aux fils des preux! ye sons of fame!
  Think of your fathers' ashes now!
Fight! for the honor of your name;
  Fight! for your valiant sires laid low!

Aux fils des preux! red be your swords
  With many a crimson battle-stain!
Fight on! ye noble knights and lords,
  Stay not to count the warlike slain!

Aux fils des preux! full many a heart
  The silent prayer now, low, is breathing,
Who with fond hopes saw ye depart;
  Fair hands the victor's crown are wreathing!

Aux fils des preux! On! soldiers, on!
　Your blades are keen, your courage strong!
Soon shall the conqueror's meed be won,
　And triumph swell our battle-song!
　　　"Aux fils des preux!"

THE BATTLE OF BLENHEIM.

ROBERT SOUTHEY.

It was a summer's evening,
　Old Kaspar's work was done,
And he before his cottage door
　Was sitting in the sun;
And by him sported on the green
His little grandchild Wilhelmine.

She saw her brother Peterkin
　Roll something large and round,
Which he beside the rivulet,
　In playing there, had found.
He came to ask what he had found,
That was so large, and smooth, and round.

Old Kaspar took it from the boy,
　Who stood expectant by;
And then the old man shook his head,
　And with a natural sigh,
"'Tis some poor fellow's skull," said he,
"Who fell in the great victory!

"I find them in the garden,
  For there's many hereabout;
And often when I go to plough
  The ploughshare turns them out;
For many thousand men," said he,
"Were slain in that great victory!"

"Now, tell us what 'twas all about,"
  Young Peterkin he cries;
And little Wilhelmine looks up
  With wonder-waiting eyes;
"Now, tell us all about the war,
And what they killed each other for?"

"It was the English," Kaspar cried,
  "Who put the French to rout;
But what they killed each other for
  I could not well make out.
But everybody said," quoth he,
"That 'twas a famous victory!

"My father lived at Blenheim then,
  Yon little stream hard by:
They burned his dwelling to the ground,
  And he was forced to fly;
So with his wife and child he fled,
Nor had he where to rest his head.

"With fire and sword the country round
  Was wasted far and wide;
And many a childing mother then
  And new-born baby died.

But things like that, you know, must be
At every famous victory.

"They say it was a shocking sight
   After the field was won;
For many thousand bodies here
   Lay rotting in the sun.
But things like that, you know, must be
After a famous victory.

"Great praise the Duke of Marlborough won,
   And our good Prince Eugene."
"Why, 'twas a very wicked thing!"
   Said little Wilhelmine.
"Nay, nay, my little girl," quoth he,
"It was a famous victory!

"And everybody praised the Duke
   Who this great fight did win."
"But what good came of it at last?"
   Quoth little Peterkin.
"Why, that I cannot tell," said he,
"But 'twas a famous victory!"

THE STAR-SPANGLED BANNER.

Francis Scott Key.

O! say, can you see, by the dawn's early light,
   What so proudly we hailed at the twilight's last
      gleaming;

Whose broad stripes and bright stars, through the per-
    ilous fight,
  O'er the ramparts we watched, were so gallantly
    streaming?
And the rockets' red glare, the bombs bursting in air,
Gave proof through the night that our flag was still
    there;
O! say, does that star-spangled banner yet wave
O'er the land of the free and the home of the brave?

On the shore, dimly seen through the mists of the deep,
  Where the foe's haughty host in dread silence reposes,
What is that which the breeze o'er the towering steep
  As it fitfully blows, half conceals, half discloses?
Now it catches the gleam of the morning's first beam;
Its full glory reflected now shines on the stream:
'Tis the star-spangled banner, O! long may it wave
O'er the land of the free and the home of the brave.

And where is the band who so vauntingly swore
  'Mid the havoc of war and the battle's confusion
A home and a country they'd leave us no more
  Their blood hath washed out their foul footsteps'
    pollution;
No refuge could save the hireling and slave
From the terror of flight, or the gloom of the grave;
And the star-spangled banner in triumph doth wave
O'er the land of the free and the home of the brave.

O! thus be it ever, when freemen shall stand
  Between our loved home and the war's desolation;

Bless'd with victory and peace, may the heaven-rescued
    land
  Praise the power that hath made and preserved us a
    nation !
Then conquer we must, for our cause it is just,
And this be our motto, " In GOD is our trust " ;
And the star-spangled banner in triumph shall wave
O'er the land of the free and the home of the brave.

MONTEREY.

CHARLES FENNO HOFFMAN.

WE were not many — we who stood
    Before the iron sleet that day —
Yet many a gallant spirit would
Give half his years if he but could
    Have been with us at Monterey.

Now here, now there, the shot, it hailed
    In deadly drifts of fiery spray,
Yet not a single soldier quailed
When wounded comrades round them wailed
    Their dying shout at Monterey.

And on — still on our column kept
    Through walls of flame its withering way;
Where fell the dead, the living stept,
Still charging on the guns that swept
    The slippery streets of Monterey.

The foe himself recoiled aghast,
  When, striking where he strongest lay,
We swooped his flanking batteries past
And braving full their murderous blast
  Stormed home the towers of Monterey.

Our banners on those turrets wave,
  And there our evening bugles play;
Where orange boughs above their grave
Keep green the memory of the brave
  Who fought and fell at Monterey.

We are not many — we who pressed
  Beside the brave who fell that day;
But who of us has not confessed
He'd rather share their warrior rest,
  Than not have been at Monterey?

THE SOLDIER'S DREAM.

Thomas Campbell.

Our bugles sang truce, for the night-cloud had lowered,
  And the sentinel stars set their watch in the sky;
And thousands had sunk on the ground overpowered,
  The weary to sleep, and the wounded to die.

When reposing that night on my pallet of straw,
  By the wolf-scaring fagot that guarded the slain,
At the dead of the night a sweet vision I saw,
  And thrice ere the morning I dreamed it again.

Methought, from the battle-field's dreadful array,
    Far, far I had roamed on a desolate track;
'Twas autumn, — and sunshine arose on the way
    To the home of my fathers, that welcomed me back.

I flew to the pleasant fields, traversed so oft
    In life's morning march, when my bosom was young;
I heard my own mountain-goats bleating aloft,
    And knew the sweet strain that the corn-reapers sung.

Then pledged we the wine-cup, and fondly I swore
    From my home and my weeping friends never to
        part;
My little ones kissed me a thousand times o'er,
    And my wife sobbed aloud in her fulness of heart.

"Stay, stay with us, — rest, thou art weary and worn!"
    And fain was their war-broken soldier to stay, —
But sorrow returned with the dawning of morn,
    And the voice in my dreaming ear melted away.

YE MARINERS OF ENGLAND.

THOMAS CAMPBELL.

Ye mariners of England,
    That guard our native seas,
Whose flag has braved a thousand years
    The battle and the breeze!
Your glorious standard launch again
    To match another foe!

And sweep through the deep,
While the stormy tempests blow;
While the battle rages loud and long,
And the stormy tempests blow.

The spirits of your fathers
Shall start from every wave!
For the deck it was their field of fame,
And ocean was their grave.
Where Blake and mighty Nelson fell
Your manly hearts shall glow
As ye sweep through the deep,
While the stormy tempests blow;
While the battle rages loud and long,
And the stormy tempests blow.

Britannia needs no bulwark,
No towers along the steep;
Her march is o'er the mountain-waves,
Her home is on the deep.
With thunders from her native oak
She quells the floods below,
As they roar on the shore,
When the stormy tempests blow;
When the battle rages loud and long,
And the stormy tempests blow.

The meteor flag of England
Shall yet terrific burn;
Till danger's troubled night depart,
And the star of peace return.

Then, then, ye ocean warriors!
Our song and feast shall flow
To the fame of your name,
When the storm has ceased to blow;
When the fiery fight is heard no more,
And the storm has ceased to blow!

SOUND THE LOUD TIMBREL.

MIRIAM'S SONG. THOMAS MOORE.

SOUND the loud timbrel o'er Egypt's dark sea!
Jehovah has triumphed, — his people are free!
Sing, — for the pride of the tyrant is broken,
   His chariots, his horsemen, all splendid and brave, —
How vain was their boasting! the Lord hath but spoken,
   And chariots and horsemen are sunk in the wave.
Sound the loud timbrel o'er Egypt's dark sea!
Jehovah has triumphed, — his people are free!

Praise to the Conqueror, praise to the Lord!
His word was our arrow, his breath was our sword.
Who shall return to tell Egypt the story
   Of those she sent forth in the hour of her pride?
For the Lord hath looked out from his pillar of glory,
   And all her brave thousands are dashed in the tide.
Sound the loud timbrel o'er Egypt's dark sea!
Jehovah hath triumphed, — his people are free!

FIFE AND DRUM.

John Dryden. Extract from "The Ode on St. Cecilia's Day."

The trumpet's loud clangor
Excites us to arms,
With shrill notes of anger
And mortal alarms.

The double, double, double beat
Of the thundering drum,
Cries, "Hark! the foes come;
Charge, charge! 'tis too late to retreat."

HOLIDAYS AND HOLY DAYS.

THE VIRGIN AT THE TEMPLE.   TITIAN.   VENICE.

HOLIDAYS AND HOLY·DAYS.

GOOD TIDINGS.

Saint Luke.

AND there were in the same country Shepherds abiding in the field, keeping watch over their flocks by night. And, lo, the Angel of the Lord came upon them, and the glory of the Lord shone round about them: and they were sore afraid. And the Angel said unto them, "Fear not, for behold I bring you good tidings of great joy, which shall be to all people.

"For unto you is born this day, in the city of David, a Saviour which is Christ the Lord. And this shall be a sign unto you; Ye shall find the babe wrapped in swaddling clothes, lying in a manger." And suddenly there was with the Angel a multitude of the heavenly host praising God and saying "Glory to God in the highest, and on earth peace, good will toward men."

WHILE SHEPHERDS WATCHED THEIR FLOCKS BY NIGHT.

NAHUM TATE.

WHILE shepherds watched their flocks by night,
   All seated on the ground,
The angel of the Lord came down,
   And glory shone around.

"Fear not," said he, for mighty dread
   Had seized their troubled mind;
"Glad tidings of great joy I bring
   To you and all mankind.

"To you, in David's town this day,
   Is born of David's line
A Saviour, who is Christ the Lord,
   And this shall be the sign.

"The heavenly babe you there shall find
   To human view displayed,
All meanly wrapped in swaddling bands,
   And in a manger laid."

Thus spake the seraph, and forthwith
   Appeared a shining throng
Of angels praising God, and thus
   Addressed their joyful song: —

"All glory be to God on high,
   And to the earth be peace!
Good-will henceforth from heaven to men
   Begin, and never cease."

CHRISTMAS CAROL.

OLD ENGLISH.

As Joseph was a-walking,
  He heard an angel sing,
"This night shall be the birthnight
  Of Christ our heavenly King.

"His birth-bed shall be neither
  In housen nor in hall,
Nor in the place of paradise,
  But in the oxen's stall.

"He neither shall be rockèd
  In silver nor in gold,
But in the wooden manger
  That lieth in the mould.

"He neither shall be washen
  With white wine nor with red,
But with the fair spring water
  That on you shall be shed.

"He neither shall be clothèd
  In purple nor in pall,
But in the fair, white linen
  That usen babies all."

As Joseph was a-walking,
  Thus did the angel sing,
And Mary's son at midnight
  Was born to be our King.

Then be you glad, good people,
　At this time of the year;
And light you up your candles,
　For His star it shineth clear.

CHRISTMAS BELLS.

JOHN KEBLE. EXTRACT.

WAKE me to-night, my mother dear,
That I may hear
The Christmas Bells, so soft and clear,
To high and low glad tidings tell,
How God the Father loved us well;
How God the Eternal Son
Came to undo what we had done.

CHRISTMAS.

ANONYMOUS.

ONCE in Royal David's city
　Stood a lowly cattle shed,
Where a mother laid her baby
　In a manger for His bed.
Mary was that mother mild,
Jesus Christ that little child.

He came down to earth from Heaven,
　Who is God and Lord of all.

And his shelter was a stable,
  And his cradle was a stall.
With the poor and mean and lowly,
Lived on earth our Saviour Holy.

And our eyes at last shall see Him
  Through His own redeeming love,
For that child so dear and gentle
  Is our Lord in Heaven above;
And He leads His children on
To the place where He is gone.

Not in that poor, lowly stable,
  With the oxen standing by,
We shall see Him; but in Heaven,
  Set at God's right hand on high,
When, like stars, His children crowned
All in white, shall wait around.

A DESIRE.

Adelaide A. Procter. Arranged.

Oh, to have dwelt in Bethlehem,
  When the star of the Lord shone bright!
To have sheltered the holy wanderers
  On that blessed Christmas night;
To have kissed the tender, way-worn feet
  Of the Mother undefiled,
And with reverent wonder and deep delight
  To have tended the holy child!

Hush! such a glory was not for thee,
    But that care may still be thine;
For are there not little ones still to aid
    For the sake of the child divine?
Are there no wandering pilgrims now,
    To thy heart and thy home to take?
And are there no mothers whose weary hearts
    You can comfort for Mary's sake?

CHRISTMAS CAROL.

FELICIA HEMANS.

O LOVELY voices of the sky,
    That hymned the Saviour's birth!
Are ye not singing still on high,
    Ye that sang, "Peace on earth"?
To us yet speak the strains,
    Wherewith, in days gone by,
Ye blessed the Syrian swains,
    O voices of the sky!

O clear and shining light, whose beams
    That hour heaven's glory shed
Around the palms, and o'er the streams,
    And on the shepherd's head;
Be near through life and death,
    As in that holiest night
Of Hope, and Joy, and Faith,
    O clear and shining light!

O star which led to Him, whose love
  Brought down man's ransom free,
Where art thou?—'midst the hosts above,
  May we still gaze on thee?
In heaven thou art not set;
  Thy rays earth might not dim;—
Send them to guide us yet!
  O star which led to Him!

A CHRISTMAS CAROL.

DINAH MARIA MULOCK.

GOD rest ye, merry gentlemen! let nothing you
    dismay,
For Jesus Christ, our Saviour, was born on Christmas
    Day.

The dawn rose red o'er Bethlehem, the stars shone
    through the gray,
When Jesus Christ, our Saviour, was born on Christmas
    Day.

God rest ye, little children; let nothing you affright,
For Jesus Christ, your Saviour, was born this happy
    night;

Along the hills of Galilee the white flocks sleeping
    lay,
When Christ, the Child of Nazareth, was born on
    Christmas Day.

God rest ye, all good Christians; upon this blessed
    morn
The Lord of all good Christians was of a woman born.

Now all your sorrows He doth heal, your sins He
    takes away;
For Jesus Christ, our Saviour, was born on Christmas
    Day.

A CHRISTMAS CAROL.

CHRISTINA G. ROSSETTI. ARRANGED.

In the bleak mid-winter
    Frosty wind made moan,
Earth stood hard as iron,
    Water like a stone;
Snow had fallen, snow on snow,
    Snow on snow,
In the bleak mid-winter
    Long ago.

Our God, Heaven cannot hold him
    Nor earth sustain;
Heaven and earth shall flee away,
    When he comes to reign.
In the bleak mid-winter
    A stable-place sufficed
The Lord God Almighty,
    Jesus Christ.

Angels and archangels
    May have gathered there;

Cherubim and seraphim
    Thronged the air.
But only His Mother,
    In her maiden bliss,
Worshipped her Beloved
    With a kiss.

What can I give Him,
    Poor as I am?
If I were a shepherd
    I would bring a lamb;
If I were a wise man,
    I would do my part, —
Yet what I can I give Him,
    Give my heart.

CHRISTMAS CAROL.

OLD ENGLISH.

LISTEN, lordings, unto me, a tale I will you tell;
Which, as on this night of glee, in David's town befell.
Joseph came from Nazareth with Mary, that sweet
    maid;
Weary were they nigh to death, and for a lodging
    prayed.

In the inn they found no room; a scanty bed they
    made;
Soon a babe, an angel pure, was in the manger laid.

Forth He came, as light through glass, He came to
  save us all.
In the stable, ox and ass before their Maker fall.

Shepherds lay afield that night to keep the silly sheep,
Hosts of angels in their sight came down from Heaven's
  high steep : —
Tidings! tidings unto you! to you a child is born,
Purer than the drops of dew, and brighter than the
  morn!

Onward then the angels sped, the shepherds onward
  went, —
God was in His manger bed; in worship low they bent.
In the morning see ye mind, my masters one and all,
At the altar Him to find, who lay within the stall.

> *Chorus.*   Sing high, sing low,
>   Sing to and fro,
>   Go tell it out with speed,
>   Cry out and shout,
>   All round about,
>   That Christ is born indeed !

THE CHRISTMAS HOLLY.

Eliza Cook.

The holly! the holly! oh, twine it with bay —
  Come give the holly a song;
For it helps to drive stern winter away,
  With his garment so sombre and long;

It peeps through the trees with its berries of red,
   And its leaves of burnished green,
When the flowers and fruits have long been dead,
   And not even the daisy is seen.
Then sing to the holly, the Christmas holly,
   That hangs over peasant and king;
While we laugh and carouse 'neath its glittering boughs,
   To the Christmas holly we'll sing.

The gale may whistle, the frost may come
   To fetter the gurgling rill;
The woods may be bare, and warblers dumb,
   But holly is beautiful still.
In the revel and light of princely halls
   The bright holly branch is found;
And its shadow falls on the lowliest walls,
   While the brimming horn goes round.

The ivy lives long, but its home must be
   Where graves and ruins are spread;
There's beauty about the cypress tree,
   But it flourishes near the dead;
The laurel the warrior's brow may wreathe,
   But it tells of tears and blood;
I sing the holly, and who can breathe
   Aught of that that is not good?
Then sing to the holly, the Christmas holly,
   That hangs over peasant and king;
While we laugh and carouse 'neath its glittering boughs,
   To the Christmas holly we'll sing.

OLD CHRISTMAS.

Mary Howitt.

Now he who knows old Christmas,
   He knows a carle of worth;
For he is as good a fellow
   As any upon earth.

He comes warm cloaked and coated,
   And buttoned up to the chin,
And soon as he comes a-nigh the door
   We open and let him in.

We know that he will not fail us,
   So we sweep the hearth up clean;
We set him in the old arm-chair,
   And a cushion whereon to lean.

And with sprigs of holly and ivy
   We make the house look gay,
Just out of an old regard to him,
   For it was his ancient way.

He must be a rich old fellow:
   What money he gives away!
There is not a lord in England
   Could equal him any day.

Good luck unto old Christmas,
   And long life, let us sing,
For he doth more good unto the poor
   Than many a crownèd king!

TO THE FIR–TREE.

TRANSLATED BY THE EDITORS. FROM THE GERMAN.

O FIR-TREE green! O Fir-tree green!
   Your leaves are constant ever,
Not only in the summer time,
But through the winter's snow and rime
   You're fresh and green forever.

O Fir-tree green! O Fir-tree green!
   I still shall love you dearly!
How oft to me on Christmas night
Your laden boughs have brought delight.
O Fir-tree green! O Fir-tree green!
   I still shall love you dearly.

A VISIT FROM ST. NICHOLAS.

CLEMENT C. MOORE.

'TWAS the night before Christmas, when all through the
   house
Not a creature was stirring, not even a mouse.
The stockings were hung by the chimney with care,
In hopes that St. Nicholas soon would be there.
The children were nestled all snug in their beds,
While visions of sugar-plums danced in their heads;
And mamma in her kerchief, and I in my cap,
Had just settled our brains for a long winter's nap —
When out on the lawn there arose such a clatter
I sprang from my bed to see what was the matter.

Away to the window I flew like a flash,
Tore open the shutter, and threw up the sash.
The moon on the breast of the new-fallen snow
Gave a lustre of midday to objects below;
When what to my wondering eyes should appear
But a miniature sleigh and eight tiny reindeer,
With a little old driver, so lively and quick,
I knew in a moment it must be St. Nick!
More rapid than eagles his coursers they came,
And he whistled and shouted and called them by name.
"Now, Dasher! now, Dancer! now, Prancer and Vixen!
On, Comet! on, Cupid! on, Donder and Blitzen! —
To the top of the porch, to the top of the wall,
Now, dash away, dash away, dash away all!"
As dry leaves that before the wild hurricane fly,
When they meet with an obstacle mount to the sky,
So, up to the housetop the coursers they flew,
With a sleigh full of toys — and St. Nicholas, too.
And then, in a twinkling, I heard on the roof
The prancing and pawing of each little hoof.
As I drew in my head, and was turning around,
Down the chimney St. Nicholas came with a bound:
He was dressed all in fur from his head to his foot,
And his clothes were all tarnished with ashes and soot:
A bundle of toys he had flung on his back,
And he looked like a pedler just opening his pack.
His eyes, how they twinkled! his dimples, how merry!
His cheeks were like roses, his nose like a cherry;
His droll little mouth was drawn up like a bow,
And the beard on his chin was as white as the snow.

The stump of a pipe he held tight in his teeth,
And the smoke, it encircled his head like a wreath.
He had a broad face and a little round belly
That shook, when he laughed, like a bowl full of jelly.
He was chubby and plump — a right jolly old elf:
And I laughed when I saw him, in spite of myself;
A wink of his eye, and a twist of his head,
Soon gave me to know I had nothing to dread.
He spoke not a word, but went straight to his work,
And filled all the stockings: then turned with a jerk,
And laying his finger aside of his nose,
And giving a nod, up the chimney he rose.
He sprang to his sleigh, to his team gave a whistle,
And away they all flew like the down of a thistle.
But I heard him exclaim, ere they drove out of sight,
"Happy Christmas to all, and to all a good-night!"

NEW YEAR'S EVE.

Hans Christian Andersen.

LITTLE Gretchen, little Gretchen wanders up and down
        the street;
The snow is on her yellow hair, the frost is at her feet,
The rows of long, dark houses without look cold and
        damp,
By the struggling of the moonbeam, by the flicker of
        the lamp.
The clouds ride fast as horses, the wind is from the
        north,

But no one cares for Gretchen, and no one looketh forth.
Within those dark, damp houses are merry faces bright,
And happy hearts are watching out the old year's latest
     night.
The board is spread with plenty where the smiling
     kindred meet,
But the frost is on the pavement and the beggar's
     in the street.

With the little box of matches she could not sell all day,
And the thin, thin tattered mantle the wind blows
     every way,
She clingeth to the railing, she shivers in the gloom, —
There are parents sitting snugly by the firelight in the
     room ;
And children with grave faces are whispering one
     another
Of presents for the New Year, for father or for mother.
But no one talks to Gretchen, and no one hears her
     speak,
No breath of little whispers comes warmly to her cheek.

No little arms are round her ; ah me ! that there should
     be,
With so much happiness on earth, so much of misery !
Sure they of many blessings should scatter blessings
     round,
As laden boughs in autumn fling their ripe fruits to the
     ground ;
And the best love man can offer to the God of love, be
     sure,

Is kindness to his little ones, and bounty to his poor.
Little Gretchen, little Gretchen goes coldly on her way;
There's no one looketh out at her, there's no one bids
    her stay.

Her home is cold and desolate; no smile, no food, no
    fire,
But children clamorous for bread, and an impatient sire.
So she sits down in an angle where two great houses
    meet,
And she curleth up beneath her, for warmth, her little
    feet;
And she looketh on the cold wall, and on the colder sky,
And wonders if the little stars are bright fires up on
    high.
She hears a clock strike slowly, up in a far church
    tower,
With such a sad and solemn tone, telling the midnight
    hour.

And she remembered her of tales her mother used to tell,
And of the cradle-songs she sang, when summer's twi-
    light fell;
Of good men and of angels, and of the Holy Child,
Who was cradled in a manger, when winter was most
    wild;
Who was poor, and cold, and hungry, and desolate and
    lone;
And she thought the song had told he was ever with
    his own;

And all the poor and hungry and forsaken ones are
　　his, —
"How good of him to look on me in such a place as
　　this!"

Colder it grows, and colder, but she does not feel it now,
For the pressure at her heart, and the weight upon her
　　brow;
But she struck one little match on the wall so cold and
　　bare,
That she might look around her, and see if He were
　　there.
The single match has kindled, and by the light it threw
It seemed to little Gretchen the wall was rent in two;
And she could see the room within, the room all warm
　　and bright,
With the fire-glow, red and dusky, and the tapers all
　　alight.
And there were kindred seated at a table richly spread
With heaps of goodly viands, red wine and pleasant
　　bread.

She could smell the fragrant savor, she could hear what
　　they did say,
Then all was darkness once again, the match had
　　burned away.
She struck another hastily, and now she seemed to see,
Within the same warm chamber, a glorious Christmas-
　　tree.
The branches were all laden with things that children
　　prize,

Bright gifts for boy and maiden, — she saw them with
    her eyes.
And she almost seemed to touch them and to hear the
    welcome shout,
When darkness fell around her, for the little match was
    out.

Another, yet another she tried — they would not light,
Till all her little store she took, and struck with all her
    might;
And the whole miserable place was lighted with the
    glare,
And lo! there stood a little child before her in the air.
There were blood-drops on his forehead, a spear-wound
    in his side,
And cruel nail-prints in his feet, and in his hands spread
    wide;
And he looked upon her gently, and she felt that he had
    known
Pain, hunger, cold, and sorrow — ay, equal to her own.

And he pointed to the laden board and to the Christmas-
    tree,
Then up to the cold sky, and said, "Will Gretchen come
    with me?"
The poor child felt her pulses fail, she felt her eyeballs
    swim,
A ringing sound was in her ears, like her dead mother's
    hymn;
And she folded both her thin white hands, and turned
    from that bright board

And from the golden gifts, and said, "With thee, with
 thee, O Lord!"
The chilly winter morning breaks up in the dull skies
On the city wrapped in vapor, on the spot where
 Gretchen lies.

In her scant and tattered garments, with her back
 against the wall,
She sitteth cold and rigid, she answers to no call.
They have lifted her up fearfully, they shuddered as
 they said,
"It was a bitter, bitter night! the child is frozen dead!"
The angels sang their greeting to one more redeemed
 from sin;
Men said, "It was a bitter night: would no one take
 her in?"
And they shivered as they spoke of her, and sighed;
 they could not see
How much of happiness there was with so much
 misery!

THANKSGIVING DAY.

Henry Alford. "Harvest-Home."

Come, ye thankful people, come,
Raise the song of Harvest-home!
All is safely gathered in,
Ere the winter storms begin;
God, our Maker, doth provide
For our wants to be supplied;

Come to God's own temple, come;
Raise the song of Harvest-home!

What is earth but God's own field,
Fruit unto his praise to yield?
Wheat and tares therein are sown,
Unto joy or sorrow grown;
Ripening with a wondrous power,
Till the final Harvest-hour:
Grant, O Lord of life, that we
Holy grain and pure may be.

Come, then, Lord of Mercy, come,
Bid us sing the Harvest-home!
Let thy saints be gathered in!
Free from sorrow, free from sin;
All upon the golden floor
Praising thee forevermore;
Come, with thousand angels, come;
Bid us sing thy Harvest-home.

EPIPHANY.

BISHOP HEBER.

BRIGHTEST and best of the sons of the morning!
  Dawn on our darkness, and lend us Thine aid,
Star of the East, the horizon adorning,
  Guide where our Infant Redeemer is laid!

Cold on His cradle the dewdrops are shining,
 Low lies His head with the beasts of the stall:
Angels adore Him in slumber reclining —
 Maker, and Monarch, and Saviour of all!

Say, shall we yield him, in costly devotion,
 Odors of Edom, and offerings divine —
Gems of the mountain, and pearls of the ocean,
 Myrrh from the forest, and gold from the mine?

Vainly we offer each ample oblation,
 Vainly with gifts would His favor secure,
Richer by far is the heart's adoration,
 Dearer to God are the prayers of the poor.

Brightest and best of the sons of the morning!
 Dawn on our darkness, and lend us Thine aid,
Star of the East, the horizon adorning,
 Guide where our Infant Redeemer is laid!

THANKSGIVING DAY.

LYDIA MARIA CHILD.

OVER the river and through the wood,
 To grandfather's house we go;
  The horse knows the way
  To carry the sleigh
Through the white and drifted snow.

Over the river and through the wood —
  Oh, how the wind does blow!
    It stings the toes
    And bites the nose,
  As over the ground we go.

Over the river and through the wood,
  To have a first-rate play.
    Hear the bells ring,
    "Ting-a-ling-ding!"
  Hurrah for Thanksgiving Day!

Over the river and through the wood
  Trot fast, my dapple-gray!
    Spring over the ground,
    Like a hunting-hound!
  For this is Thanksgiving Day.

Over the river and through the wood,
  And straight through the barn-yard gate.
    We seem to go
    Extremely slow, —
  It is so hard to wait!

Over the river and through the wood —
  Now grandmother's cap I spy!
    Hurrah for the fun!
    Is the pudding done?
  Hurrah for the pumpkin-pie!

APRIL FOOLS.

WILLIAM PRAED.

THIS day, beyond all contradiction,
This day is all thine own, Queen Fiction!
And thou art building castles boundless
Of groundless joys, and griefs as groundless;
Assuring beauties that the border
Of their new dress is out of order;
And schoolboys that their shoes want tying;
And babies that their dolls are dying.
　　Lend me, lend me some disguise;
　　I will tell prodigious lies;
　　All who care for what I say
　　Shall be April fools to-day.

THE MAY QUEEN.

ALFRED TENNYSON.

YOU must wake and call me early, call me early,
　　mother dear;
To-morrow'll be the happiest time of all the glad New
　　year;
Of all the glad New year, mother, the maddest merriest
　　day;
For I'm to be Queen o' the May, mother, I'm to be
　　Queen o' the May.

There's many a black, black eye, they say, but none so
　　bright as mine;

There 's Margaret and Mary, there 's Kate and Caroline;
But none so fair as little Alice, in all the land, they say,
So I'm to be Queen o' the May, mother, I'm to be
    Queen o' the May.

I sleep so sound all night, mother, that I shall never
    wake,
If you do not call me loud when the day begins to
    break ;
But I must gather knots of flowers, and buds and
    garlands gay,
For I'm to be Queen o' the May, mother, I'm to be
    Queen o' the May.

As I came up the valley whom think ye should I see,
But Robin leaning on the bridge beneath the hazel-tree?
He thought of that sharp look, mother, I gave him yes-
    terday —
But I'm to be Queen o' the May, mother, I'm to be
    Queen o' the May.

He thought I was a ghost, mother, for I was all in
    white
And I ran by him without speaking, like a flash of
    light.
They call me cruel-hearted, but I care not what they
    say,
For I'm to be Queen o' the May, mother, I'm to be
    Queen o' the May.

They say he 's dying all for love, but that can never be:

They say his heart is breaking, mother — but what is
    that to me?
There 's many a bolder lad'll woo me any summer day,
And I'm to be Queen o' the May, mother, I'm to be
    Queen o' the May.

Little Effie shall go with me to-morrow to the green,
And you 'll be there, too, mother, to see me made the
    Queen;
For the shepherd lads on every side'll come from far
    away,
And I'm to be Queen o' the May, mother, I'm to be
    Queen o' the May.

The honeysuckle round the porch has wov'n its wavy
    bowers,
And by the meadow-trenches blow the faint sweet
    cuckoo-flowers;
And the wild marsh-marigold shines like fire in swamps
    and hollows gray,
And I'm to be Queen o' the May, mother, I'm to be
    Queen o' the May.

The night winds come and go, mother, upon the
    meadow-grass,
And the happy stars above them seem to brighten as
    they pass;
There will not be a drop of rain the whole of the live-
    long day,
And I'm to be Queen o' the May, mother, I'm to be
    Queen o' the May.

All the valley, mother, 'll be fresh and green and still,
And the cowslip and the crowfoot are over all the hill,
And the rivulet in the flowery dale'll merrily glance
         and play,
For I'm to be Queen o' the May, mother, I'm to be
         Queen o' the May.

So you must wake and call me early, call me early,
         mother dear,
To-morrow'll be the happiest time of all the glad New
         year;
To-morrow'll be of all the year the maddest merriest
         day,
For I'm to be Queen o' the May, mother, I'm to be
         Queen o' the May.

FAIRY FOLK AND FABLE.

CHERUBS AT PLAY.   CORREGGIO.   PARMA.

FAIRY FOLK AND FABLE.

ARIEL'S SONG.

WILLIAM SHAKESPEARE.

WHERE the bee sucks there suck I;
In a cowslip's bell I lie;
There I couch when owls do cry;
On the bat's back I do fly
After summer merrily.
Merrily, merrily, shall I live now,
Under the blossom that hangs on the bough.

DEATH OF OBERON.

WALTER THORNBURY.

TOLL the lilies' silver bells!
  Oberon, the king, is dead!
In her grief the crimson rose
  All her velvet leaves has shed.

Toll the lilies' silver bells!
  Oberon is dead and gone!

He who looked an emperor
  When his glow-worm crown was on.

Toll the lilies' silver bells!
  Slay the dragon-fly, his steed;
Dig his grave within the ring
  Of the mushrooms in the mead.

THE MERMAID.

ALFRED TENNYSON.

WHO would be,
A mermaid fair,
Singing alone,
Combing her hair
Under the sea,
In a golden curl
With a comb of pearl,
On a throne?

I would be a mermaid fair;
I would sing to myself the whole of the day;
With a comb of pearl I would comb my hair;
And still as I combed I would sing and say,
"Who is it loves me? who loves not me?"
I would comb my hair till my ringlets would fall
Low adown, low adown,
From under my starry sea-bud crown
Low adown and around,

And I should look like a fountain of gold
Springing alone
With a shrill inner sound,
Over the throne
In the midst of the hall.

THE FORSAKEN MERMAN.

MATTHEW ARNOLD.

COME, dear children, let us away;
   Down and away below.
Now my brothers call from the bay;
Now the great winds shorewards blow;
Now the salt tides seawards flow;
Now the wild white horses play,
Champ and chafe and toss in the spray
   Children dear, let us away.
     This way, this way.

Call her once before you go.
   Call once yet,
In a voice that she will know:
   "Margaret! Margaret!"

Children's voices should be dear
(Call once more) to a mother's ear:
Children's voices wild with pain.
   Surely she will come again.
Call her once, and come away.
     This way, this way.

"Mother dear, we cannot stay."
The wild white horses foam and fret,
    Margaret! Margaret!

Come, dear children, come away down.
    Call no more.
One last look at the white-walled town,
And the little gray church on the windy shore,
    Then come down.
She will not come though you call all day.
    Come away, come away.

Children dear, was it yesterday
We heard the sweet bells over the bay?
    In the caverns where we lay,
    Through the surf and through the swell,
The far-off sound of a silver bell?
Sand-strewn caverns cool and deep,
Where the winds are all asleep;
Where the spent lights quiver and gleam;
Where the salt weed sways in the stream;
Where the sea-beasts rang'd all round
Feed in the ooze of their pasture ground;
Where the sea-snakes coil and twine,
Dry their mail and bask in the brine;
Where great whales come sailing by,
Sail and sail, with unshut eye,
Round the world forever and aye?
    When did music come this way?
    Children dear, was it yesterday?

Children dear, was it yesterday
(Call yet once) that she went away?
Once she sat with you and me,
    On a red gold throne in the heart of the sea.
    And the youngest sat on her knee.
She comb'd its bright hair, and she tended it well,
When down swung the sound of the far-off bell,
She sigh'd, she look'd up through the clear green
    sea,
She said, "I must go, for my kinsfolk pray
In the little gray church on the shore to-day.
'Twill be Easter-time in the world — ah me!
And I lose my poor soul, Merman, here with thee."
I said, "Go up, dear heart, through the waves:
Say thy prayer, and come back to the kind sea-caves."
She smiled, she went up through the surf in the bay.
    Children dear, was it yesterday?

    Children dear, were we long alone?
"The sea grows stormy, the little ones moan;
Long prayers," I said, "in the world they say."
"Come," I said, and we rose through the surf in the
    bay.
We went up the beach in the sandy down
Where the sea-stocks bloom, to the white-walled town,
Through the narrow paved streets, where all was still
To the little gray church on the windy hill.
From the church came a murmur of folk at their
    prayers,
But we stood without in the cold blowing airs.

We climb'd on the graves on the stones worn with
  rains,
And we gazed up the aisle through the small leaded
  panes.
  She sat by the pillar; we saw her clear;
  "Margaret, hist! come quick, we are here.
  Dear heart," I said, "we are here alone.
  The sea grows stormy, the little ones moan."
But, ah, she gave me never a look,
For her eyes were seal'd to the holy book.
  "Loud prays the priest; shut stands the door."
Come away, children, call no more,
Come away, come down, call no more.

  Down, down, down,
  Down to the depths of the sea,
She sits at her wheel in the humming town,
   Singing most joyfully.
Hark what she sings: "O joy, O joy,
From the humming street, and the child with its toy,
From the priest and the bell, and the holy well,
  From the wheel where I spun,
  And the blessed light of the sun."
  And so she sings her fill,
  Singing most joyfully,
  Till the shuttle falls from her hand,
  And the whizzing wheel stands still.
She steals to the window and looks at the sand;
  And over the sand at the sea;
  And her eyes are set in a stare;

And anon there breaks a sigh,
And anon there drops a tear,
From a sorrow clouded eye,
And a heart sorrow laden,
    A long, long sigh,
For the cold strange eyes of a little Mermaiden,
And the gleam of her golden hair.

Come away, away, children,
Come children, come down.
The hoarse wind blows colder;
Lights shine in the town.
She will start from her slumber
When gusts shake the door;
She will hear the winds howling,
Will hear the waves roar.
We shall see, while above us
The waves roar and whirl,
A ceiling of amber,
A pavement of pearl.
Singing, "Here came a mortal,
But faithless was she,
And alone dwell forever
The kings of the sea."

But, children, at midnight,
When soft the winds blow,
When clear falls the moonlight,
When spring-tides are low;
When sweet airs come seaward
From heaths starr'd with broom;

And high rocks throw mildly
On the blanch'd sands a gloom:
Up the still, glistening beaches,
Up the creeks we will hie;
Over banks of bright seaweed
The ebb-tide leaves dry.
We will gaze from the sand-hills
At the white sleeping town;
At the church on the hillside —
    And then come back, down.
Singing, "There dwells a loved one,
But cruel is she:
She left lonely forever
The kings of the sea."

THE FAIRY FOLK.

WILLIAM ALLINGHAM.

Up the airy mountain,
    Down the rushy glen
We daren't go a-hunting,
    For fear of little men;
Wee folk, good folk,
    Trooping all together;
Green jacket, red cap,
    And white owl's feather.

Down along the rocky shore
    Some make their home,
They live on crispy pancakes

Of yellow tide-foam;
Some in the reeds
  Of the black mountain-lake,
With frogs for their watch-dogs,
  All night awake.

High on the hill-top
  The old King sits;
He is now so old and gray
  He's nigh lost his wits.
With a bridge of white mist
  Columbkill he crosses,
On his stately journeys
  From Slieveleague to Rosses;
Or going up with music,
  On cold starry nights,
To sup with the Queen
  Of the gay Northern Lights.

They stole little Bridget
  For seven years long;
When she came down again
  Her friends were all gone.
They took her lightly back,
  Between the night and morrow;
They thought that she was fast asleep,
  But she was dead with sorrow.
They have kept her ever since
  Deep within the lakes,
On a bed of flag leaves,
  Watching till she wakes.

By the craggy hillside,
   Through the mosses bare,
They have planted thorn-trees
   For pleasure here and there.
Is any man so daring
   As dig one up in spite?
He shall find the thornies set
   In his bed at night.

Up the airy mountain,
   Down the rushy glen,
We daren't go a-hunting
   For fear of little men;
Wee folk, good folk,
   Trooping all together;
Green jacket, red cap,
   And white owl's feather.

FAIRY SONG.

JOHN KEATS.

SHED no tear! O shed no tear!
The flower will bloom another year.
Weep no more! O weep no more!
Young buds sleep in the roots' white core.
Dry your eyes! O dry your eyes!
For I was taught in Paradise
To ease my breast of melodies —
                Shed no tear!

Overhead! look overhead!
'Mong the blossoms white and red —
Look up, look up! I flutter now
On this fresh pomegranate bough.
See me! 'tis this silvery bill
Ever cures the good man's ill.
Shed no tear! O shed no tear!
The flower will bloom another year.
Adieu, adieu — I fly — adieu!
I vanish in the heaven's blue —

Adieu, adieu!

THE WOUNDED DAISY.

Anonymous.

A fairy was mending a daisy
  Which some one had torn in half;
Her sisters all thought her crazy,
  And only looked on to laugh.
They showed her scores in the hedges,
  And scores that grew by the tarn,
And scores on the green field-edges,
  But she went on with her darn.

Then round they cluster, and chatter —
  How each had a flower more fine;
One shook buttercups at her,
  And one brought briony-twine,
Strong red poppies to vex her,
  Tiny bright-eyes to beguile,

Tall green flags to perplex her;
　　But she worked on all the while.

She work'd and she sang this ditty,
　　While insects wondered and heard;
(They knew by the tone of pity
　　The song was not from a bird):
"Daisy, somebody hurt you!
　　Are you afraid of me?
Patient hope is a virtue,
　　Wait and you shall see!

"Was it a careless mower
　　Cut your blossom in twain?
I hope his hand will be slower
　　When he sees you again.
Was it a step unheeding?
　　Or was it a stormy gale?
Or was it — (*how* you are bleeding!)
　　A dark, malicious snail?

"They did not know you would suffer,
　　I think they had never seen;
Slugs and snails may be rougher,
　　Perhaps, than they always mean.
Do I not hear one sobbing,
　　Down just there at my foot?
Or is it only the throbbing
　　Down in your poor little root?

"Ah, you tremble a little!
　　Have I hurt you at last?

If you were not so brittle,
  I could mend you so fast.
No; there's nothing distressful,
  Only a quiver of bliss, —
Daisy, I've been successful!
  Grow, and give me a kiss!

"Now I've mended you neatly,
  All the fairies can see;
Now you look at me sweetly,
  Are you grateful to me?
I'll go hiding behind you,
  Then in a day or two,
Perhaps a baby will find you,
  And I shall hear it coo.

"Yes, your cheeks may be whiter
  Than the rest of your race;
Other eyes may be brighter,
  Others fairer in face;
But no flower that uncloses
  Can be precious as you,
Not an army of roses
  Fighting all the year through!"

Then the fairies confess it,
  As that daisy revives;
All come round and caress it,
  All so glad that it lives.
No one ventures to doubt it,
  Hosts of penitent fays

Make their dance-rings about it,
   Sing their songs in its praise.

Years of fading and growing
   Pass,— the daisy is not!
Sweeter grass-blooms are growing
   Still by that little spot.
There each fairy that hover'd
   Sang while pausing above,
" Here the daisy recover'd, —
   Here is a footprint of Love! "

THE LITTLE FAY.

ROBERT BUCHANAN. EXTRACT.

WHEN the summer day
Makes the greenwood gay
   And the blue sky clear,
I roam wherever I may
   And I feel no fear.

I rise from my bed of an acorn cup
   And shake the dew from my hair and eyes,
Then I stoop to a dewdrop and drink it up,
   And it seems to strengthen my wings to rise.
     Then I fly, I fly!
     I rise up high,
   High as the greenwood tree.

The humming bee and the butterfly
And the moth with its broad brown wings go by

While down on the leaf of an oak I lie,
    Covered up where none can see !
But I seem to hear strange voices call
Like the hum of a distant waterfall
    Sighing and saddening me.
And still I lie and hearken there,
Swinging and floating high in air;
And the voices make me red and pale
    Till the sunbeams go,
And the large green fly with his silken sail
    Floats by me slow,
And the leaves grow dark and are lightly rolled,
The soft boughs flutter, the dews fall cold,
    And the shadows grow
    Before I know !
And down I fall to the side of the stream,
And with palpitating silver gleam
    I see it flow
As the moon comes out above the place,
And I stoop to drink, and smile to trace
The water-kelpie's cold, strange face
    Gleaming below.

QUEEN MAB.

Thomas Hood.

A little fairy comes at night,
    Her eyes are blue, her hair is brown,
With silver spots upon her wings,
    And from the moon she flutters down.

She has a little silver wand,
   And when a good child goes to bed,
She waves her wand from right to left
   And makes a circle round its head.

And then it dreams of pleasant things,
   Of fountains filled with fairy fish,
And trees that bear delicious fruit
   And bow their branches at a wish.

Of arbors filled with dainty scents
   From lovely flowers that never fade;
Bright flies that glitter in the sun,
   And glow-worms shining in the shade;

And singing-birds with gifted tongues
   For singing songs and telling tales;
And pretty dwarfs to show the way
   Through fairy hills and fairy dales.

But when a bad child goes to bed,
   From left to right she weaves her rings,
And then it dreams all through the night
   Of only ugly, horrid things!

Then lions come with glaring eyes,
   And tigers growl — a dreadful noise;
And ogres draw their cruel knives
   To shed the blood of girls and boys.

Then stormy waves rush on to drown,
   And raging flames come scorching round;

Fierce dragons hover in the air,
  And serpents crawl along the ground.

Then wicked children wake and weep
  And wish the long, black gloom away;
But good ones love the dark, and find
  The night as pleasant as the day.

THE FAIRIES OF THE CALDON–LOW.

MARY HOWITT.

"AND where have you been, my Mary,
  And where have you been from me?"
"I've been to the top of the Caldon-Low,
  The midsummer night to see!"

"And what did you see, my Mary,
  All up on the Caldon-Low?"
"I saw the blithe sunshine come down,
  And I saw the merry winds blow."

"And what did you hear, my Mary,
  All up on the Caldon Hill?"
"I heard the drops of water made,
  And I heard the corn-ears fill."

"Oh tell me all, my Mary —
  All, all that ever you know;
For you must have seen the fairies
  Last night on the Caldon-Low."

"Then take me on your knee, mother,
  And listen, mother of mine :
A hundred fairies danced last night,
  And the harpers they were nine;

"And merry was the glee of the harp-strings,
  And their dancing feet so small;
But oh! the sound of their talking
  Was merrier far than all!"

"And what were the words, my Mary,
  That you did hear them say?"
"I'll tell you all, my mother,
  But let me have my way.

"And some they played with the water
  And rolled it down the hill;
'And this,' they said, 'shall speedily turn
  The poor old miller's mill;

"'For there has been no water
  Ever since the first of May;
And a busy man shall the miller be
  By the dawning of the day!

"'Oh, the miller, how he will laugh,
  When he sees the mill-dam rise!
The jolly old miller, how he will laugh,
  Till the tears fill both his eyes!'

"And some they seized the little winds,
  That sounded over the hill,

And each put a horn into his mouth,
  And blew so sharp and shrill!

"'And there,' said they, 'the merry winds go,
  Away from every horn;
And those shall clear the mildew dank
  From the blind old widow's corn:

"'Oh, the poor blind widow —
  Though she has been blind so long,
She'll be merry enough when the mildew's gone,
  And the corn stands stiff and strong!'

"And some they brought the brown linseed,
  And flung it down from the Low:
'And this,' said they, 'by the sunrise,
  In the weaver's croft shall grow!

"'Oh, the poor lame weaver!
  How will he laugh outright
When he sees his dwindling flax-field
  All full of flowers by night!'

"And then upspoke a brownie,
  With a long beard on his chin;
'I have spun up all the tow,' said he,
  'And I want some more to spin.

"'I've spun a piece of hempen cloth,
  And I want to spin another —
A little sheet for Mary's bed
  And an apron for her mother.'

"And with that I could not help but laugh,
　　And I laughed out loud and free;
And then on the top of the Caldon-Low,
　　There was no one left but me.

"And all on the top of the Caldon-Low
　　The mists were cold and gray,
And nothing I saw but the mossy stones
　　That round about me lay.

"But, as I came down from the hill-top,
　　I heard, afar below,
How busy the jolly miller was,
　　And how merry the wheel did go!

"And I peeped into the widow's field,
　　And, sure enough, was seen
The yellow ears of the mildewed corn
　　All standing stiff and green!

"And down by the weaver's croft I stole,
　　To see if the flax were high;
But I saw the weaver at his gate
　　With the good news in his eye!

"Now, this is all that I heard, mother,
　　And all that I did see;
So, prithee, make my bed, mother,
　　For I'm tired as I can be!"

THE FAIRY TO PUCK.

WILLIAM SHAKESPEARE.

OVER hill, over dale,
Thorough bush, thorough briar,
Over park, over pale,
Thorough flood, thorough fire,
I do wander every where,
  Swifter than the moone's sphere.
And I serve the Fairy Queen,
To dew her orbs upon the green;
The cowslips tall her pensioners be,
In their gold coats spots you see, —
Those be rubies, Fairy favours:
In those freckles live their savours.
I must go seek some dew-drops here,
And hang a pearl in every cowslip's ear.

SONG OF THE ELFIN MILLER.

ALLAN CUNNINGHAM.

FULL merrily rings the millstone round,
  Full merrily rings the wheel,
Full merrily gushes out the grist —
  Come, taste my fragrant meal!
As sends the lift its snowy drift,
  So the meal comes in a shower;
Work, fairies, fast, for time flies past —
  I borrowed the mill an hour.

The miller he's a worldly man,
   And maun hae double fee;
So draw the sluice of the churl's dam,
   And let the stream come free.
Shout, fairies, shout! see, gushing out,
   The meal comes like a river:
The top of the grain on hill and plain
   Is ours, and shall be ever.

One elf goes chasing the wild bat's wing
   And one the white owl's horn;
One hunts the fox for the white o' his tail
   And we winna hae him till morn.
One idle fay, with the glow-worm's ray,
   Runs glimmering 'mong the mosses;
Another goes tramp wi' the will-o-wisps' lamp,
   To light a lad to the lasses.

O haste, my brown elf, bring me corn
   From Bonnie Blackwood plains;
Go, gentle fairy, bring me grain
   From green Dalgona mains;
But, pride of a' at Closeburn ha',
   Fair is the corn and fatter;
Taste, fairies, taste, a gallanter grist
   Has never been wet with water.

Hilloah! my hopper is heaped high;
   Hark to the well-hung wheels!
They sing for joy; the dusty roof
   It clatters and it reels.

Haste, elves, and turn yon mountain burn —
  Bring streams that shine like siller;
The dam is down, the moon sinks soon,
  And I maun grind my miller.

Ha! bravely done, my wanton elves,
  That is a foaming stream:
See how the dust from the mill flies,
  And chokes the cold moon-beam.
Haste, fairies, fleet come baptized feet,
  Come sack and sweep up clean,
And meet me soon, ere sinks the moon,
  In thy green vale, Dalreen.

THE LARCH AND THE OAK.

Thomas Carlyle.

"What is the use of thee, thou gnarled sapling?" said
a young larch-tree to a young oak. "I grow three feet
in a year, thou scarcely so many inches; I am straight
and taper as a reed, thou straggling and twisted as a
loosened withe." — "And thy duration," answered the
oak, "is some third part of man's life and I am ap-
pointed to flourish for a thousand years. Thou art
felled and sawed into paling, where thou rottest and
art burned after a single summer; of me are fashioned
battle-ships, and I carry mariners and heroes into unknown seas."

The richer a nature the harder and slower its development. Two boys were once of a class in the Edinburgh grammar-school: John ever trim, precise, and dux; Walter ever slovenly, confused, and dolt. In due time John became Baillie John of Hunter-Square, and Walter became Sir Walter Scott of the Universe.

The quickest and completest of all vegetables is the cabbage.

THE MOUNTAIN AND THE SQUIRREL.

R. W. EMERSON.

THE Mountain and the Squirrel
Had a quarrel,
And the former called the latter "Little Prig,"
Bun replied:
"You are doubtless very big;
But all sorts of things and weather
Must be taken in together
To make up a year,
And a sphere;
And I think it no disgrace
To occupy my place.
If I'm not so large as you,
You're not so small as I,
And not half so spry;
I'll not deny you make
A very pretty squirrel track.
Talents differ; all is well and wisely put;
If I cannot carry forests on my back,
Neither can you crack a nut."

THE LARK AND THE ROOK.

ANONYMOUS.

"GOOD-NIGHT, Sir Rook!" said a little lark,
"The daylight fades; it will soon be dark;
I've bathed my wings in the sun's last ray,
I've sung my hymn to the parting day;
So now I haste to my quiet nook
In yon dewy meadow — good-night, Sir Rook!"

"Good-night, poor Lark," said his titled friend,
With a haughty toss and a distant bend;
"I also go to my rest profound,
But not to sleep on the cold, damp ground:
The fittest place for a bird like me
Is the topmost bough of yon tall pine-tree.

"I opened my eyes at peep of day
And saw you taking your upward way,
Dreaming your fond romantic dreams,
An ugly speck in the sun's bright beams,
Soaring too high to be seen or heard,
And I said to myself: 'What a foolish bird!'

"I trod the park with a princely air,
I filled my crop with the richest fare;
I cawed all day 'mid a lordly crew,
And I made more noise in the world than you!
The sun shone forth on my ebon wing;
I looked and wondered — good-night, poor thing!"

"Good-night, once more," said the lark's sweet voice,
"I see no cause to repent my choice;
You build your nest in the lofty pine,
But is your slumber more sweet than mine?
You make more noise in the world than I,
But whose is the sweeter minstrelsy?"

THE GOOSE WITH THE GOLDEN EGGS.

ÆSOP.

A CERTAIN man had the good fortune to possess a goose which laid him a golden egg every day. But dissatisfied with so slow an income, and thinking to seize the whole treasure at once, he killed the goose and, cutting her open, found her just what any other goose would be.

Much wants more and loses all.

THE CAMEL'S NOSE.

LYDIA H. SIGOURNEY.

ONCE in his shop a workman wrought,
With languid head and listless thought,
When, through the open window's space,
Behold, a camel thrust his face!
"My nose is cold," he meekly cried,
"Oh, let me warm it by thy side!"

Since no denial word was said,
In came the nose, in came the head:
As sure as sermon follows text,
The long and scraggy neck came next;
And then, as falls the threatening storm,
In leaped the whole ungainly form.

Aghast, the owner gazed around,
And on the rude invader frowned,
Convinced, as closer still he pressed,
There was no room for such a guest;
Yet more astonished, heard him say,
"If thou art troubled, go away,
For in this place I choose to stay."

O youthful hearts to gladness born,
Treat not this Arab lore with scorn!
To evil habits' earliest wile
Lend neither ear, nor glance, nor smile;
Choke the dark fountain ere it flows,
Nor e'en admit the camel's nose!

THE WOODPECKER AND THE DOVE.

TRANSLATED BY EDITORS. FROM THE GERMAN.

A WOODPECKER and a Dove had been visiting a Peacock. "How did you like our host?" asked the Woodpecker after they had left. "Is he not a disagreeable creature? His vanity, his shapeless feet, his horrid voice, are unbearable, aren't they?"

"I had no time," answered the gentle dove, "to notice these things," I was so occupied with the beauty of his head, the gorgeousness of his colors, and the majesty of his train."

THE DEW–DROP.

RICHARD C. TRENCH.

A DEW-DROP, falling on the ocean-wave,
Exclaimed, in fear, "I perish in this grave!"
But, in a shell received, that drop of dew
Unto a pearl of marvellous beauty grew;
And, happy now, the grace did magnify
Which thrust it forth — as it had feared — to die;
Until again, "I perish quite!" it said,
Torn by rude diver from its ocean bed:
O, unbelieving! — So it came to gleam
Chief jewel in a monarch's diadem.

THE MISER AND HIS THREE SONS.

GOLDSMITH.

POOR Dick, the happiest silly fellow I ever knew, was of the number of those good-natured creatures that are said to do no harm to any but themselves. Whenever he fell into any misery, he called it "seeing life." If his head was broken by a chairman, or his pocket picked by a sharper, he comforted himself by imitating the Hibernian dialect of the one, or the more fashionable cant of the other. Nothing came amiss to him.

Although the eldest of three sons, his inattention to money matters had incensed his father to such a degree that all intercession of friends was fruitless. The old gentleman was on his death-bed. The whole family (and Dick among the number) gathered around him. "I leave my second son Andrew," said the expiring miser, "my whole estate; and desire him to be frugal." "Ah! father," said Andrew, in a sorrowful tone (as is usual on these occasions), "may heaven prolong your life and health to enjoy it yourself."

"I recommend Simon, my third son, to the care of his elder brother; and leave him, besides, four thousand pounds." "Ah! father," cried Simon (in great affliction, to be sure), "may heaven give you life and health to enjoy it yourself!"

At last, turning to poor Dick, "As for you, you have always been a sad dog; you'll never come to good; you'll never be rich; I leave you a shilling to buy a halter." "Ah! father," cries Dick, without any emotion, "*may heaven give you life and health to enjoy it yourself!*"

THE GOURD AND THE PALM.

A Persian Fable.

"How old art thou?" said the garrulous gourd,
As o'er the palm-tree's crest it poured
Its spreading leaves and tendrils fine,

And hung a bloom in the morning shine.
"A hundred years!" the palm-tree sighed:
"And *I*," the saucy gourd replied,
"Am at the most a hundred hours,
And overtop thee in the bowers!"

Through all the palm-tree's leaves there went
A tremor as of self-content.
"I live my life," it whispering said,
"See what I see, and count the dead;
And every year, of all I've known,
A gourd above my head has grown,
And made a boast, like thine to-day;
Yet here *I* stand — but where are *they?*"

THE EAR OF CORN.

TRANSLATED BY THE EDITORS. FROM THE GERMAN.

A FARMER went with his little son into the field one day to see if the corn were ripe. "See, father," said the boy, "how high these ears hold their heads, they are surely ripe, but those that bow down almost to the ground must be bad."

The father picked two ears and said: "Foolish child, look here. These ears that hold up their heads so proudly are dry and withered, these that bow down are the finest corn."

When the head is held too high
The brains inside are poor and dry.

THE SPIDER AND THE FLY.

MARY HOWITT.

"WILL you walk into my parlor?"
    Said a spider to a fly;
"'Tis the prettiest little parlor
    That ever you did spy.
The way into my parlor
    Is up a winding stair,
And I have many pretty things
    To show when you are there."
"Oh no, no!" said the little fly,
    "To ask me is in vain;
For who goes up your winding stair
    Can ne'er come down again."

"I'm sure you must be weary
    With soaring up so high;
Will you rest upon my little bed?"
    Said the spider to the fly.
"There are pretty curtains drawn around,
    The sheets are fine and thin;
And if you like to rest awhile,
    I'll snugly tuck you in."
"Oh no, no!" said the little fly,
    "For I've often heard it said,
They never, never wake again
    Who sleep upon your bed."

Said the cunning spider to the fly,
    "Dear friend, what shall I do

To prove the warm affection
  I've always felt for you?
I have, within my pantry,
  Good store of all that's nice;
I'm sure you're very welcome —
  Will you please to take a slice?"
"Oh no, no!" said the little fly,
  "Kind sir, that cannot be;
I've heard what's in your pantry,
  And I do not wish to see."

"Sweet creature," said the spider,
  "You're witty and you're wise;
How handsome are your gauzy wings!
  How brilliant are your eyes!
I have a little looking-glass
  Upon my parlor shelf;
If you'll step in one moment, dear,
  You shall behold yourself."
"I thank you, gentle sir," she said,
  "For what you're pleased to say,
And bidding you good-morning, now,
  I'll call another day."

The spider turned him round about,
  And went into his den,
For well he knew the silly fly
  Would soon be back again;
So he wove a subtle thread
  In a little corner sly,

And set his table ready
  To dine upon the fly.
He went out to his door again,
  And merrily did sing,
"Come hither, hither, pretty fly,
  With the pearl and silver wing;
Your robes are green and purple,
  There's a crest upon your head;
Your eyes are like the diamond bright,
  But mine are dull as lead."

Alas, alas! how very soon
  This silly little fly,
Hearing his wily, flattering words,
  Came slowly flitting by:
With buzzing wings she hung aloft,
  Then near and nearer drew —
Thought only of her brilliant eyes,
  And green and purple hue;
Thought only of her crested head, —
  Poor foolish thing! At last
Up jumped the cunning spider,
  And fiercely held her fast.

He dragged her up his winding stair,
  Into his dismal den,
Within his little parlor — but
  She ne'er came out again.
And now, dear little children
  Who may this story read,

To idle, silly, flattering words,
 I pray you, ne'er give heed.
Unto an evil counsellor
 Close heart and ear and eye,
And take a lesson from this tale
 Of the spider and the fly.

JUPITER AND THE BEE.

Æsop.

In days of yore when the world was young, a Bee that had stored her combs with a beautiful harvest, flew up to heaven to present as a sacrifice an offering of honey. Jupiter was so delighted with the gift that he promised to give her whatsoever she should ask for. She therefore besought him saying, "O glorious Jove, maker and master of every poor Bee, give thy servant a sting, that when any one approaches my hive to take the honey I may kill him on the spot."

Jupiter, out of love to man, was angry at her request and thus answered her: "Your prayer shall not be granted in the way you wish, but the sting which you ask for you shall have; and when any one comes to take away your honey and you attack him, the wound shall be fatal not to him but to you, for your life shall go with your sting."

He that prays harm for his neighbor, begs a curse upon himself.

THE FLYING–FISH.

FLORIAN. TRANSLATION OF J. W. PHELPS.

A FLYING-FISH, tired of her lot,
Unto her mother thus complained,
"You may be pleased, but I am not,
To live forever thus constrained.
I cannot leap into the air
But what the eagle's waiting there;
And if I dive into the sea,
The dolphin there is after me."
The dame replied, in accents mild,
"I've found in this strange world, my child,
And now must let you know,
That medium folks, as you and I,
Should not aspire to soar too high,
Nor seek to dive too low."

THE FOX AND THE CROW.

JANE TAYLOR.

To a dairy a crow,
Having ventured to go,
Some food for her young ones to seek,
Flew up to the trees,
With a fine piece of cheese,
Which she joyfully held in her beak.

A fox, who lived by,
To the tree saw her fly,

And to share in the prize made a vow;
> For having just dined,
> He for cheese felt inclined,
So he went and sat under the bough.

She was cunning, he knew,
> But so was he too,
And with flattery adapted his plan;
> For he knew if she'd speak,
> It must fall from her beak,
So, bowing politely, began.

"'Tis a very fine day:"
> (Not a word did she say;)
"The wind, I believe, ma'am, is south;
> A fine harvest for peas:"
> He then look'd at the cheese,
But the crow did not open her mouth.

Sly Reynard, not tired,
> Her plumage admired,
"How charming! how brilliant its hue!
> The voice must be fine,
> Of a bird so divine,
Ah, let me just hear it, pray do.

"Believe me, I long
> To hear a sweet song."
The silly crow foolishly tries:
> She scarce gave one squall,
> When the cheese she let fall,
And the fox ran away with the prize.

Ye innocent fair,
Of coxcombs beware,
To flattery never give ear :
Try well each pretence,
And keep to plain sense,
And then you have little to fear.

THE ANT AND THE CRICKET.

ANONYMOUS.

A silly young cricket, accustomed to sing
Through the warm, sunny months of gay summer and
    spring,
Began to complain, when he found that at home
His cupboard was empty and winter was come.
    Not a crumb to be found
    On the snow-covered ground ;
    Not a flower could he see,
    Not a leaf on a tree :
"Oh, what will become," says the cricket, "of me?"

At last by starvation and famine made bold,
All dripping with wet and all trembling with cold,
Away he set off to a miserly ant,
To see if, to keep him alive, he would grant
    Him shelter from rain :
    A mouthful of grain
    He wished only to borrow,
    He'd repay it to-morrow :
If not, he must die of starvation and sorrow.

Says the ant to the cricket, "I'm your servant and
    friend,
But we ants never borrow, we ants never lend ;
But tell me, dear sir, did you lay nothing by
When the weather was warm?" Said the cricket,
    "Not I.
            My heart was so light
            That I sang day and night,
            For all nature looked gay."
        "You *sang*, sir, you say?
Go then," said the ant, "and *dance* winter away."

Thus ending, he hastily lifted the wicket
And out of the door turned the poor little cricket.
Though this is a fable, the moral is good :
If you live without work, you must live without food.

THE WIND AND THE SUN.

ÆSOP.

A DISPUTE once arose between the Wind and the Sun
which was the stronger of the two, and they agreed to
put the point upon this issue : that whichever soonest
made a traveller take off his cloak should be accounted
the more powerful. The Wind began, and blew with all
his might and main a blast, cold and fierce as a Thra-
cian storm ; but the stronger he blew the closer the
traveller wrapped his cloak around him and the tighter
he grasped it with his hands. Then broke out the Sun :

with his welcome beams he dispersed the vapor and the cold; the traveller felt the genial warmth, and as the sun shone brighter and brighter he sat down, overcome with the heat, and cast his cloak on the ground.

Thus the Sun was declared the conqueror, and it has ever been deemed that persuasion is better than force.

THE NIGHTINGALE AND THE GLOWWORM.

William Cowper.

A NIGHTINGALE that all day long
Had cheered the village with his song,
Nor yet at eve his note suspended,
Nor yet when eventide was ended,
Began to feel, as well he might,
The keen demands of appetite;
When looking eagerly around,
He spied far off, upon the ground,
A something shining in the dark,
And knew the glowworm by his spark;
So, stooping down from hawthorn top,
He thought to put him in his crop.

The worm, aware of his intent,
Harangued him thus, right eloquent:
"Did you admire my lamp," quoth he,
"As much as I your minstrelsy,
You would abhor to do me wrong,
As much as I to spoil your song:

For 'twas the self-same Power Divine
Taught you to sing, and me to shine;
That you with music, I with light,
Might beautify and cheer the night."
The songster heard this short oration,
And warbling out his approbation,
Released him, as my story tells,
And found a supper somewhere else.

THE IDLE MAGNET.

TRANSLATED BY THE EDITORS. FROM THE GERMAN.

A BOY had a magnet. He wanted to keep it new and nice, so he put it into a chest away from all other iron. By and by he took it out to use. He held it to a piece of iron, but the magnet would not work any more because in its idleness it had lost all its strength.

THE COUNTRY MAID AND HER MILK CAN.

ÆSOP.

A COUNTRY maid was walking along with a can of milk upon her head when she fell into the following train of reflections. "The money for which I shall sell this milk will enable me to increase my stock of eggs to three hundred. These eggs, allowing for what may prove addle and what may be destroyed by vermin will produce at least two hundred and fifty chickens.

The chickens will be fit to carry to market just at the time when poultry is always dear; so that by the new year I cannot fail of having money enough to purchase a new gown. Green — let me consider — yes, green becomes my complexion best, and green it shall be. In this dress I will go to the fair, where all the young fellows will strive to have me for a partner; but no — I shall refuse every one of them, and with a disdainful toss turn from them." Transported with this idea she could not forbear acting with her head the thought that thus passed in her mind; when down came the can of milk! and all her imaginary happiness vanished in a moment.

Do not count your chickens before they are hatched.

BAUCIS AND PHILEMON.

JONATHAN SWIFT.

In ancient times, as story tells,
The saints would often leave their cells,
And stroll about, but hide their quality,
To try good people's hospitality.

It happened on a winter night,
As authors of the legend write,
Two brother hermits, saints by trade,
Taking their tour in masquerade,
Disguised in tattered habits went
To a small village down in Kent;
Where, in the stroller's canting strain,

They begged from door to door in vain,
Tried every tone might pity win;
But not a soul would take them in.

Our wandering saints, in woful state,
Treated at this ungodly rate,
Having through all the village passed,
To a small cottage came at last
Where dwelt a good old honest yeoman,
Call'd in the neighborhood Philemon;
Who kindly did these saints invite
In his poor hut to pass the night;
And then the hospitable sire
Bid goody Baucis mend the fire;
While he from out the chimney took
A flitch of bacon off the hook,
And freely from the fattest side
Cut out large slices to be fried;
Then stepped aside to fetch them drink,
Filled a large jug up to the brink,
And saw it fairly twice go round;
Yet (what is wonderful!) they found
'Twas still replenished to the top,
As if they ne'er had touched a drop.
The good old couple were amazed,
And often on each other gazed;
For both were frightened to the heart,
And just began to cry, "What art!"
Then softly turned aside to view
Whether the lights were burning blue.

"Good folks, you need not be afraid,
We are but saints," the hermits said;
"No hurt shall come to you or yours:
But for that pack of churlish boors,
Not fit to live on Christian ground,
They and their houses shall be drowned;
Whilst you shall see your cottage rise,
And grow a church before your eyes."

They scarce had spoke, when fair and soft
The roof began to mount aloft,
Aloft rose every beam and rafter,
The heavy wall climbed slowly after;
The chimney widened and grew higher,
Became a steeple with a spire.

The kettle to the top was hoist,
And there stood fastened to a joist;
Doomed ever in suspense to dwell,
'Tis now no kettle, but a bell.
A wooden jack which had almost
Lost by disuse the art to roast,
A sudden alteration feels,
Increased by new intestine wheels;
The jack and chimney, near allied,
Had never left each other's side:
The chimney to a steeple grown,
The jack would not be left alone;
But up against the steeple reared,
Became a clock, and still adhered.

The groaning chair began to crawl,
Like a huge snail, along the wall;
There stuck aloft in public view,
And with small change a pulpit grew.
The cottage, by such feats as these,
Grown to a church by just degrees,
The hermits then desired the host
To ask for what he fancied most.
Philemon, having paused awhile,
Returned them thanks in homely style:
" I'm old, and fain would live at ease;
Make me the parson, if you please."

Thus happy in their change of life
Were several years this man and wife.
When on a day, which proved their last,
Discoursing on old stories past,
They went by chance, amidst their talk,
To the churchyard to take a walk;
When Baucis hastily cried out,
" My dear, I see your forehead sprout!"
" But yes! Methinks, I feel it true;
And really yours is budding too —
Nay, — now I cannot stir my foot;
It feels as if 'twere taking root!"
Description would but tire my muse;
In short, they both were turned to yews.

THE FARTHING RUSHLIGHT.

Æsop.

A RUSHLIGHT that had grown fat and saucy with too much grease boasted one evening before a large company that it shone brighter than the sun, the moon, and all the stars. At that moment a puff of wind came and blew it out. One who lighted it again said " Shine on, friend Rushlight, and hold your tongue; the lights of heaven are never blown out."

NURSERY RHYMES AND CRADLE SONGS.

PORTRAIT OF A CHILD OF CHARLES I.   VAN DYCK.

NURSERY RHYMES.

A BABY'S FEET.

ALGERNON CHARLES SWINBURNE.

A BABY'S feet, like sea-shells pink,
 Might tempt, should heaven see meet,
An angel's lips to kiss, we think, —
 A baby's feet.

Like rose-hued sea-flowers toward the heat
 They stretch and spread and wink
Their ten soft buds that part and meet.

No flower-bells that expand and shrink
 Gleam half so heavenly sweet,
As shine on life's untrodden brink, —
 A baby's feet.

A BABY'S HANDS.

ALGERNON CHARLES SWINBURNE.

A BABY'S hands, like rosebuds furled,
 Whence yet no leaf expands,
Ope if you touch, though close upcurled, —
 A baby's hands.

Then, even as warriors grip their brands
　　When battle's bolt is hurled,
They close, clenched hard like tightening bands.

No rosebuds yet by dawn impearled
　　Match, even in loveliest lands,
The sweetest flowers in all the world, —
　　A baby's hands.

NAE SHOON.

ANONYMOUS.

Nae shoon to hide her tiny tae,
　　Nae stocking on her feet;
Her supple ankles white as snaw,
　　Like early blossoms sweet.

Her simple dress of sprinkled pink,
　　Her double, dimpled chin,
Her puckered lips and balmy mou',
　　Wi' nae one tooth between.

Her e'en sae like her mither's e'en, —
　　Twa gentle, liquid things;
Her face is like an angel's face, —
　　We're glad she has nae wings.

She is the budding of our love,
　　A giftie God's gied us;
We munna love the gift o'erweel,
　　'Twad be nae blessing thus.

INFANT JOY.

WILLIAM BLAKE.

"I HAVE no name,
I am but two days old."
What shall I call thee?
"I happy am,
Joy is my name."
Sweet joy befall thee!

Pretty joy!
Sweet joy but two days old!
Sweet joy I call thee.
Thou dost smile,
I sing the while.
Sweet joy befall thee!

A CHILL.

CHRISTINA G. ROSSETTI.

WHAT can lambkins do
All the keen night through?
Nestle by their woolly mother,
The careful ewe.

What can nestlings do
In the nightly dew?
Sleep beneath their mother's wing,
Till day breaks anew.

If in field or tree
There might only be
Such a warm, soft sleeping-place
Found for me!

THE LAMB.

WILLIAM BLAKE.

LITTLE lamb, who made thee?
Dost thou know who made thee,
Gave thee life and bade thee feed
By the stream and o'er the mead;
Gave thee clothing of delight,
Softest clothing, woolly, bright;
Gave thee such a tender voice,
Making all the vales rejoice?
Little lamb, who made thee?

Dost thou know who made thee?
Little lamb, I'll tell thee;
Little lamb, I'll tell thee.
He is callèd by thy name,
For He calls himself a Lamb.
He is meek and He is mild,
He became a little child.
I a child and thou a lamb,
We are callèd by His name.
Little lamb, God bless thee!
Little lamb, God bless thee!

THE LITTLE ANGEL.

ELIZABETH PRENTISS.

RIGHT into our house one day
  A dear little angel came;
I ran to him, and said softly,
  "Little angel, what is your name?"

He said not a word in answer,
  But smiled a beautiful smile;
Then I said, "May I go home with you?
  Shall you go in a little while?"

But Mamma said, "Dear little angel,
  Don't leave us; oh, always stay!
We will all of us love you dearly;
  Sweet angel, oh, *don't* go away!"

So he staid and he staid, and we love him
  As we could not have loved another.
Do you want to know what his name is?
  His name is — *my little brother!*

CHILD'S SONG.

ALGERNON CHARLES SWINBURNE.

WHAT is gold worth, say,
Worth for work or play,
Worth to keep or pay,

Hide or throw away,
    Hope about or fear?
What is love worth, pray?
    Worth a tear?

Golden on the mould
Lie the dead leaves rolled
Of the wet woods old,
Yellow leaves and cold,
    Woods without a dove.
Gold is worth but gold;
    Love's worth love.

A LITTLE BRAWL.

Translation of Mary Howitt.   From the Swedish of F. Bremer.

At times a little brawl
    Injures not at all,
If we only love each other still.
    Cloudy heaven clears
    Itself and bright appears,
For such is Nature's will.

The heart within its cage
    Is a bird in rage,
Which doth madly strive to fly.
    Love and Truth can best
    Flatter it to rest,
Flatter it to rest right speedily.

LITTLE THINGS.

ANONYMOUS.

LITTLE drops of water,
Little grains of sand,
Make the mighty ocean
And the pleasant land.

Thus the little minutes,
Humble though they be,
Make the mighty ages
Of eternity.

Thus our little errors
Lead the soul away
From the path of virtue
Off in sin to stray.

Little deeds of kindness,
Little words of love,
Make this earth an Eden,
Like the heaven above.

MOTHER'S SONG.

ANONYMOUS.

DON'T grow old too fast, my sweet!
Stay a little while
In this pleasant baby-land,
Sunned by mother's smile.

Grasp not with thy dimpled hands
　At the world outside;
They are still too rosy soft,
　Life too cold and wide.

Be not wistful, sweet blue eyes!
　Find your rest in mine,
Which through life shall watchful be
　To keep all tears from thine.

Be not restless, little feet!
　Lie within my hand;
Far too round these tiny soles
　Yet to try to stand.

For awhile be mine alone,
　So helpless and so dear;
By-and-by thou must go forth,
　But now, sweet, slumber here!

FIRST FOOTSTEPS.

ALGERNON CHARLES SWINBURNE.

A LITTLE way, more soft and sweet
　Than fields aflower with May,
A babe's feet, venturing, scarce complete
　A little way.

Eyes full of dawning day
Look up for mother's eyes to meet
　Too blithe for song to say.

Glad as the golden Spring to greet
Its first live leaflet's play,
Love, laughing, leads the little feet
A little way.

THE BIRTHDAY WEEK.

Anonymous.

MONDAY'S bairn is fair in the face;
Tuesday's bairn is full of grace;
Wednesday's bairn is the child of woe;
Thursday's bairn has far to go;
Friday's bairn is loving and giving;
Saturday's bairn works hard for a living;
But the bairn that is born on the Sabbath day
Is lucky and bonny and wise and gay.

POLITENESS.

Anonymous.

POLITENESS is to do and say
The kindest thing in the kindest way.

THE GOLDEN RULE.

New England Primer.

BE you to others kind and true,
As you'd have others be to you.

SOLOMON AND MAMMA.

ANONYMOUS.

SOLOMON says, in words so mild,
"Spare the rod and spoil the child!"
My mamma thinks, as well as he,
A little whipping's good for me.

THE GOLDEN RULE.

ANONYMOUS.

To do to others as I would
　　That they should do to me,
Will make me honest, kind, and good,
　　As children ought to be.

THE BABY.

GEORGE MACDONALD.

WHERE did you come from, baby dear?
Out of the everywhere into the here.

Where did you get your eyes so blue?
Out of the sky as I came through.

What makes the light in them sparkle and spin?
Some of the starry spikes left in.

Where did you get that little tear?
I found it waiting when I got here.

What makes your forehead so smooth and high?
A soft hand stroked it as I went by.

What makes your cheek like a warm, white rose?
Something better than any one knows.

Whence that three-cornered smile of bliss?
Three angels gave me at once a kiss.

Where did you get that pearly ear?
God spoke, and it came out to hear.

Where did you get those arms and hands?
Love made itself into hooks and bands.

Feet, whence did you come, you darling things?
From the same box as the cherub's wings.

How did they all just come to be you?
God thought about me, and so I grew.

But how did you come to us, you dear?
God thought of *you*, and so I am here.

LITTLE KITTY.

Elizabeth Prentiss.

ONCE there was a little kitty,
  Whiter than snow;
In the barn she used to frolic,
  Long time ago.

In the barn a little mousie
　Ran to and fro;
For she heard the kitty coming,
　Long time ago.

Two black eyes had little kitty,
　Black as a sloe;
And they spied the little mousie,
　Long time ago.

Nine pearl teeth had little kitty,
　All in a row;
And they bit the little mousie,
　Long time ago.

When the teeth bit little mousie,
　Little mouse cried, "Oh!"
But she got away from kitty,
　Long time ago.

MILKING TIME.

CHRISTINA G. ROSSETTI.

WHEN the cows come home the milk is coming;
Honey's made while the bees are humming;
Duck and drake on the rushy lake,
And the deer live safe in the breezy brake;
And timid, funny, pert little bunny
Winks his nose, and sits all sunny.

JENNY WREN AND ROBIN REDBREAST.

OLD ENGLISH RHYME.

JENNY WREN fell sick;
  Upon a merry time,
In came Robin Redbreast
  And brought her sops of wine.

"Eat well of the sop, Jenny,
  Drink well of the wine;"
"Thank you, Robin, kindly,
  You shall be mine."

Jenny she got well,
  And stood upon her feet,
And told Robin plainly
  She loved him not a bit.

Robin, being angry,
  Hopp'd upon a twig,
Saying, "Out upon you,
  Fye upon you, bold-faced jig!"

THE OLD MARKET-WOMAN.

OLD ENGLISH RHYME.

THERE was an old woman, as I've heard tell,
She went to market her eggs for to sell;
She went to market all on a market day;
And she fell asleep on the king's highway.

There came by a pedler whose name was Stout,
He cut her petticoats all round about;
He cut her petticoats up to the knees,
Which made the old woman to shiver and freeze.

When this little woman first did wake,
She began to shiver and she began to shake,
She began to wonder and she began to cry,
"Lawk-a-mercy on me, this is none of I:

"But if it be I, as I do hope it be,
I've a little dog at home, and he'll know me;
If it be I, he'll wag his little tail,
And if it be not I, he'll loudly bark and wail!"

Home went the little woman all in the dark,
Up got the little dog, and he began to bark;
He began to bark, so she began to cry,
"Lawk-a-mercy on me, this is none of I!"

POLLY.

GEORGE MACDONALD.

BROWN eyes, straight nose;
Dirt pies, rumpled clothes.

Torn books, spoilt toys;
Arch looks, unlike a boy's;

Little rages, obvious arts;
(Three her age is), cakes, tarts;

Falling down off chairs;
Breaking crown down stairs;

Catching flies on the pane;
Deep sighs — cause not plain;

Bribing you with kisses
For a few farthing blisses.

Wide-a-wake; as you hear,
"Mercy's sake, quiet, dear!"

New shoes, new frock;
Vague views of what is o'clock

When it's time to go to bǝd,
And scorn sublime for what is said.

Folded hands, saying prayers,
Understands not nor cares —

Thinks it odd, smiles away;
Yet may God hear her pray!

Fast asleep, as you see,
Heaven keep my girl for me!

THE LOST DOLL.

CHARLES KINGSLEY.

I ONCE had a sweet little doll, dears,
  The prettiest doll in the world;
Her cheeks were so red and so white, dears,
  And her hair was so charmingly curled.

But I lost my poor little doll, dears,
   As I played on the heath one day;
And I cried for her more than a week, dears,
   But I never could find where she lay.

I found my poor little doll, dears,
   As I played on the heath one day;
Folks say she is terribly changed, dears,
   For her paint is all washed away.
And her arms trodden off by the cows, dears,
   And her hair's not the least bit curled;
Yet for *old time's sake,* she is still, dears,
   The prettiest doll in the world.

BABY BYE.

THEODORE TILTON.

BABY bye,
Here's a fly;
Let us watch him, you and I.
   How he crawls
   Up the walls,
   Yet he never falls!
I believe with six such legs
You and I could walk on eggs.
   There he goes
   On his toes,
   Tickling baby's nose.

Spots of red
Dot his head;
Rainbows on his back are spread;
 That small speck
 Is his neck;
 See him nod and beck.
I can show you, if you choose,
Where to look to find his shoes, —
 Three small pairs,
 Made of hairs;
 These he always wears.

Black and brown
Is his gown;
He can wear it upside down;
 It is laced
 Round his waist;
 I admire his taste.
Yet though tight his clothes are made,
He will lose them, I'm afraid,
 If to-night
 He gets sight
 Of the candle-light.

In the sun
Webs are spun;
What if he gets into one?
 When it rains
 He complains
 On the window-panes.
Tongue to talk have you and I;

God has given the little fly
    No such things,
    So he sings
    With his buzzing wings.

He can eat
Bread and meat;
There's his mouth between his feet.
    On his back
    Is a pack
    Like a pedler's sack.
Does the baby understand?
Then the fly shall kiss her hand;
    Put a crumb
    On her thumb,
    Maybe he will come.

Catch him? No,
Let him go,
Never hurt an insect so;
    But no doubt
    He flies out
    Just to gad about.
Now you see his wings of silk
Drabbled in the baby's milk;
    Fie, oh fie,
    Foolish fly!
    How will he get dry?

All wet flies
Twist their thighs

Thus they wipe their heads and eyes;
    Cats, you know,
    Wash just so,
    Then their whiskers grow.
Flies have hairs too short to comb,
So they fly bareheaded home;
    But the gnat
    Wears a hat,
    Do you believe that?

Flies can see
More than we.
So how bright their eyes must be!
    Little fly,
    Ope your eye;
    Spiders are near by.
For a secret I can tell, —
Spiders never use flies well.
    Then away!
    Do not stay.
    Little fly, good-day!

CRADLE SONGS.

A LULLABY.

LADY NAIRNE.

BALOO, loo, lammy, now baloo, my dear.
Does wee lammy ken that its daddy's no here?
Ye're rocking full sweetly on mammy's warm knee,
But daddy's a-rocking upon the salt sea.

Now hush-a-by, lammy, now hush-a-by, dear;
Now hush-a-by, lammy, for mother is near.
The wild wind is raving, and mammy's heart's sair;
The wild wind is raving, and ye dinna care.

Sing baloo, loo, lammy, sing baloo, my dear;
Sing baloo, loo, lammy, for mother is here.
My wee bairnie's dozing, it's dozing now fine,
And, oh, may its wakening be blither than mine!

LITTLE BIRDIE.

ALFRED TENNYSON.

WHAT does little birdie say,
In her nest at peep of day?
"Let me fly," says little birdie,
"Mother, let me fly away."

"Birdie, rest a little longer,
Till the little wings are stronger."
So she rests a little longer,
    Then she flies away.

What does little baby say,
In her bed at peep of day?
Baby says, like little birdie,
    "Let me rise and fly away."
"Baby, sleep a little longer,
Till the little limbs are stronger.
If she sleeps a little longer,
    Baby, too, shall fly away."

LULLABY.

Alfred Tennyson.

Sweet and low, sweet and low,
    Wind of the western sea,
Low, low, breathe and blow,
    Wind of the western sea!
Over the rolling waters go;
Come from the dying moon, and blow,
    Blow him again to me;
While my little one, while my pretty one, sleeps.

Sleep and rest, sleep and rest;
Father will come to thee soon.
Rest, rest on mother's breast;
    Father will come to thee soon.

Father will come to his babe in the nest;
Silver sails all out of the west,
  Under the silver moon;
Sleep, my little one, sleep, my pretty one, sleep!

CRADLE SONG.

FROM THE GERMAN.   TRANSLATED BY E. L. PRENTISS.

SLEEP, baby, sleep!
Thy father is watching the sheep!
Thy mother is shaking the dreamland tree,
And down drops a little dream for thee.
  Sleep, baby, sleep!

Sleep, baby, sleep!
The great stars are the sheep,
The little stars are the lambs, I guess;
The bright moon is the shepherdess.
  Sleep, baby, sleep!

Sleep, baby, sleep!
And cry not like a sheep,
Else the sheep-dog will bark and whine,
And bite this naughty child of mine.
  Sleep, baby, sleep!

Sleep, baby, sleep!
Thy Saviour loves His sheep;
He is the Lamb of God on high,
Who, for our sakes, came down to die.
  Sleep, baby, sleep!

Sleep, baby, sleep!
Away to tend the sheep,
Away, thou sheep-dog fierce and wild,
And do not harm my sleeping child!
Sleep, baby, sleep!

AN OLD GAELIC CRADLE-SONG.

ANONYMOUS.

Hush! the waves are rolling in,
  White with foam, white with foam:
Father toils amid the din;
  But baby sleeps at home.

Hush! the winds roar hoarse and deep!
  On they come, on they come!
Brother seeks the lazy sheep,
  But baby sleeps at home.

Hush! the rain sweeps o'er the knowes,
  Where they roam, where they roam:
Sister goes to seek the cows;
  But baby sleeps at home.

MOTHER GOOSE LULLABIES.

Hushaby, baby, thy cradle is green;
Father's a nobleman, mother's a queen;
Sister's a lady, and wears a gold ring;
Brother's a drummer, and drums for the king.

ROCKABY, baby, on the tree-top;
When the wind blows the cradle will rock;
When the bough breaks the cradle will fall;
Down will come baby and cradle and all.

By-lo, baby-bunting!
Papa's gone a-hunting;
Mamma's gone to get a skin
To wrap her baby-bunting in.

CRADLE–SONG.

R. W. GILDER.

In the embers shining bright,
A garden grows for thy delight,
With roses yellow, red, and white.

But, O my child, beware, beware!
Touch not the roses growing there,
For every rose a thorn doth bear!

WILLIE WINKIE.

WILLIAM MILLER.

WEE Willie Winkie rins through the town,
Up-stairs and doon-stairs in his nicht-gown,
Tirlin' at the window, cryin' at the lock,
"Are the weans in their bed? — for it's now ten
o'clock."

Hey, Willie Winkie, are ye comin' ben?
The cat's singin' gay thrums to the sleepin' hen,
The doug's speldered on the floor, and disna gie a
  cheep;
But here's a waukrife laddie that winna fa' asleep.

Onything but sleep, ye rogue! — glowerin' like the
  moon,
Rattlin' in an airn jug wi' an airn spoon;
Rumblin' tumblin' roun' about, crawin' like a cock,
Skirlin' like a kenna-what — wauknin' sleepin' folk.

Hey, Willie Winkie! the wean's in a creel,
Waumblin' aff a bodie's knee like a vera eel;
Ruggin' at the cat's lug, and ravellin' a' her thrums:
Hey, Willie Winkie! — See, there he comes!

Weary is the mither that has a storie wean,
A wee stumpie stoussie that canna rin his lane,
That has a battle aye wi' sleep before he'll close an ee;
But a kiss frae aff his rosy lips gies strength anew to
  me.

CUDDLE DOON.

ALEXANDER ANDERSON.

THE bairnies cuddle doon at nicht,
  Wi' muckle faucht an' din;
Oh, try an' sleep, ye waukrife rogues,
  Your father's comin' in.

They never heed a word I speak;
  I try to gie a froon,
But aye I hap them up, an' cry,
  "O bairnies, cuddle doon."

Wee Jamie wi' the curly heid —
  He aye sleeps next the wa' —
Bangs up an' cries, "I want a piece";
  The rascal starts them a'.
I rin an' fetch them pieces, drinks,
  They stop awee the soun';
Then draw the blankets up and cry,
  "Noo, weanies, cuddle doon."

But ere five minutes gang, wee Rab
  Cries oot frae 'neath the claes,
"Mither, mak' Tam gie ower at ance —
  He's kittlin' wi' his taes."
The mischief's in that Tam for tricks,
  He'd bother half the toon:
But aye I hap them up an' cry,
  "O bairnies, cuddle doon."

At length they hear their father's fit,
  An', as he steeks the door,
They turn their faces to the wa',
  While Tam pretends to snore.
"Hae a' the weans been gude?" he asks,
  As he pits off his shoon;
"The bairnies, John, are in their beds,
  An' lang since cuddled doon."

An' just afore we bed oorsel',
   We look at oor wee lambs;
Tam has his airms roun' wee Rab's neck,
   An' Rab his airms roun' Tam's.
I lift wee Jamie up the bed,
   An', as I straik each croon,
I whisper, till my heart fills up,
   "O bairnies, cuddle doon."

The bairnies cuddle doon at nicht,
   Wi' mirth that's dear to me;
But sune the big warl's cark an' care
   Will quaten doon their glee.
Yet come what will to ilka ane,
   May He who sits aboon
Aye whisper, though their pows be bauld,
   "O bairnies, cuddle doon."

I THINK WHEN I READ THAT SWEET STORY OF OLD.

JEMIMA LUKE.

I THINK, when I read that sweet story of old,
   When Jesus was here among men,
How He called little children as lambs to his fold,
   I should like to have been with Him then.

I wish that His hand had been placed on my head,
   That His arms had been thrown around me,

And that I might have heard His kind voice when
    He said,
"Let the little ones come unto me."

Yet still to His foot-stool in prayer I may go,
    And ask for a share in His love;
And if I thus earnestly seek Him below,
    I shall see Him and hear Him above,

In that beautiful home He has gone to prepare
    For all who are washed and forgiven;
And many dear children are gathering there,
    For of such is the kingdom of heaven.

TO THE GUARDIAN ANGEL.

From the French of Mme. Tastu. Translated and arranged by the Editors.

Watch over me while I'm asleep,
And, as God bids you, vigil keep;
And every night above my head
Bend down, dear Angel, o'er the bed.
Have pity on my feebleness,
Walk by my side to guard and bless;
Talk to me all along the way,
And, while I hearken what you say,
Lest I should fall, help me to stand;
I pray you, Angel, hold my hand!

CRADLE HYMN.

ISAAC WATTS.

HUSH, my dear, lie still and slumber;
    Holy angels guard thy bed;
Heavenly blessings without number
    Gently falling on thy head.

Sleep, my babe, thy food and raiment,
    House and home, thy friends provide;
All without thy care, or payment,
    All thy wants are well supplied.

Soft and easy is thy cradle;
    Coarse and hard thy Saviour lay,
When his birthplace was a stable,
    And his softest bed was hay.

May'st thou live to know and fear him,
    Trust and love him all thy days;
Then go dwell forever near him,
    See his face and sing his praise.

SHADOW–TOWN FERRY.

LILIAN DYNEVOR RICE.

SWAY to and fro in the twilight gray;
    This is the ferry of Shadow-town.
It always sails at the end of day,
    Just as the darkness is coming down.

Rest, little head, on my shoulder, so —
  A sleepy kiss is the only fare;
Drifting away from the world we go,
  Baby and I, in the rocking-chair.

See, where the fire-logs glow and spark
  Glitter the lights of the shadow-land!
The winter rains on the window — hark! —
  Are ripples lapping up its strand.

Rock slow, more slow, in the dusky light,
  Silently lower the anchor down;
Dear little passenger, say "Good-night!"
  We have reached the harbor of Shadow-town.

GOOD–NIGHT.

VICTOR HUGO. TRANSLATED AND ARRANGED BY THE EDITORS.

GOOD-NIGHT! Good-night!
Far flies the light;
But still God's love
Shall flame above,
Making all bright.
Good-night! Good-night!

ADVERTISEMENTS

STAR=LAND

Talks with Young People about the Wonders of the Heavens.

By Sir ROBERT S. BALL,
Royal Astronomer of Ireland.

Cloth. 384 pages. Fully illustrated. For introduction, $1.00.

THIS is a book of the rarest excellence. It combines the knowledge of a royal astronomer with the happy faculty of the story-teller.

It is based upon two courses of Christmas lectures delivered to children at the Royal Institution, Great Britain, and is something of rare quality, — lucid, fascinating, and yet thoroughly scientific.

This fascinating book treats, in a manner equally true to science and attractive to children, all the chief topics of Astronomy : the sun, the moon, the planets, comets, meteors, and the stars. It is just the book that has been wanted for a long time, and is calculated not only to interest and instruct, but to lead to greater effort, on the part of the learner, in the right direction.

The Right Hon. W. E. Gladstone: I have now finished reading your luminous and delightful Star-Land, and I am happy to be in a sense enrolled amongst your young pupils.

GINN & COMPANY, Publishers,
Boston.   New York.   Chicago.   Atlanta.   Dallas.

THE JANE ANDREWS BOOKS

A remarkable series of attractive and interesting books for young people, — written in a clear, easy, and picturesque style. This is the famous Jane Andrews series which has been for many years an old-time favorite with young folks. Other juvenile books come and go, but the Jane Andrews books maintain the irresistible charm they always have had.

THE SEVEN LITTLE SISTERS WHO LIVE ON THE ROUND BALL THAT FLOATS IN THE AIR. 12mo. Cloth. 143 pages. Illustrated. For introduction, 50 cents.

EACH AND ALL; THE SEVEN LITTLE SISTERS PROVE THEIR SISTERHOOD. 12mo. Cloth. Illustrated. 162 pages. For introduction, 50 cents.

THE STORIES MOTHER NATURE TOLD HER CHILDREN. 12mo. Cloth. Illustrated. 161 pages. For introduction, 50 cents.

TEN BOYS WHO LIVED ON THE ROAD FROM LONG AGO TO NOW. 12mo. Cloth. 243 pages. Illustrated. For introduction, 50 cents.

GEOGRAPHICAL PLAYS. 12mo. Cloth. 140 pages. For Introduction, 50 cents.

The "Seven Little Sisters" represent the seven races, and the book shows how people live in the various parts of the world, what their manners and customs are, what the products of each section are and how they are interchanged.

"Each and All" continues the story of Seven Little Sisters, and tells more of the peculiarities of the various races, especially in relation to childhood.

Dame Nature unfolds in "Stories Mother Nature Told" some of her most precious secrets. She tells about the amber, about the dragon-fly and its wonderful history, about water-lilies, how the Indian corn grows, what queer pranks the Frost Giants indulge in, about coral, and starfish, and coal mines, and many other things in which children take delight.

In "Ten Boys" the History of the World is summarized in the stories of Kabla the Aryan boy, Darius the Persian boy, Cleon the Greek boy, Horatius the Roman boy, Wulf the Saxon boy, Gilbert the Knight's page, Roger the English boy, Fuller the Puritan boy, Dawson the Yankee boy, and Frank Wilson the boy of 1885.

In "Ten Boys" one is struck with the peculiar excellence of its style, — clear, easy, graceful, and picturesque, — which a child cannot fail to comprehend, and in which "children of a larger growth" will find an irresistible charm. — **John G. Whittier.**

GINN & COMPANY, Publishers, Boston, New York, and Chicago.

THE CYR READERS

By ELLEN M. CYR.

THE CHILDREN'S PRIMER. Sq. 12mo. Cloth. Fully illustrated. 106 pages. For introduction, 24 cents.

THE CHILDREN'S FIRST READER. Sq. 12mo. Cloth. Fully illustrated. 111 pages. For introduction, 28 cents.

THE CHILDREN'S SECOND READER. Sq. 12mo. Cloth. Fully illustrated. 197 pages. For introduction, 36 cents.

THE CHILDREN'S THIRD READER. Sq. 12mo. Cloth. Fully illustrated. 280 pages. For introduction, 50 cents.

THE CHILDREN'S FOURTH READER. Sq. 12mo. Cloth. Fully illustrated. 388 pages. For introduction, 60 cents.

The Children's Primer contains more reading matter, in proportion to the number of new words, than any other book in the market.

The Children's First Reader is made for the second half-year. It is a simple but steady growth in the same line with the Primer.

The Children's Second Reader is based upon stories from the lives of Longfellow and Whittier, supplemented by many other pretty stories of nature and childhood.

The Children's Third Reader is arranged on the same lines as the Second Reader. Stories from the lives of Lowell, Holmes, and Bryant are introduced.

The Children's Fourth Reader has been prepared on the same lines as the Second and Third Readers. Sketches of Hawthorne, Dickens, Scott, Tennyson, and Irving are introduced, amply illustrated with portraits and pictures of the homes of these authors. Choice selections have also been made from authors whose writings are especially interesting and instructive to pupils of fourth reader grade.

GINN & COMPANY, Publishers,

Boston. New York. Chicago. Atlanta. Dallas.